CLINICAL RESEARCH ASSOCIATE JOBS FOR LIFE SCIENCE DEGREE HOLDERS, RNS, AND IMGS

A GUIDE TO SIX-FIGURE CRA INCOME IN CLINICAL RESEARCH MONITORING

J.P HOLDASHAM

WETIN BOOKS

2nd Edition

eISBN: 978-1-962798-60-0

paperback ISBN: 978-1-962798-61-7

CONTENTS

AUTHOR'S NOTE

Dear Reader,

Welcome to the updated edition of **Clinical Research Associate Jobs For Life Science Degree Holders, RNs, and IMGs**. It's been 13 years since the first edition was published, and this revised guide reflects the significant changes in the clinical research landscape since then.

The inspiration for updating this book came from the positive feedback received from readers who successfully launched CRA careers using the strategies outlined in the original edition. The success stories have been remarkable - from nurses who found new career paths with improved compensation to international medical graduates who discovered their clinical knowledge was highly valued in the research space.

Since the first edition, the clinical research landscape has transformed dramatically. The COVID-19 pandemic accelerated many changes, normalizing remote monitoring, decentralized trials, and virtual patient engagement. Despite these technological and methodological evolutions, the fundamental challenge remains: how do qualified professionals break into the field and navigate toward rewarding, six-figure careers?

This updated guide maintains the practical, straightforward approach of the original while incorporating essential information relevant to today's clinical research environment. I've intentionally kept it concise—focusing on what you need to know to get started quickly—while addressing the modern realities of the profession.

For those seeking more comprehensive information, this guide serves as a companion to my forthcoming book, **CLINICAL RESEARCH CAREERS FOR HEALTHCARE PROFESSIONALS: A Comprehensive Guide to Launching and Excelling in Clinical Research**. While this shorter book gives you the essentials to secure your first CRA position, the expanded work will provide deeper insights into the broader clinical research landscape, additional career pathways, and advanced strategies for long-term success.

The clinical research profession continues to offer extraordinary opportunities for healthcare professionals willing to position themselves strategically. I hope this guide serves as your practical roadmap to a fulfilling and financially rewarding career in this dynamic field.

Wishing you success in your clinical research journey,

J.P. Holdasham

CHAPTER 1

THE LACK OF EXPERIENCE PROBLEM

M*ost people who succeed in the face of seemingly impossible conditions are people who simply don't know how to quit.*

- Robert H. Schuller

Getting a job as a Clinical Research Associate (CRA) remains highly competitive. The industry has created a paradoxical barrier: you need relevant experience to get hired, but how can you gain that experience without first landing a position?

It is critical to understand that, as a CRA job applicant, you must demonstrate expertise and knowledge whenever you present yourself in interviews and meetings.

This raises the obvious practical question – how does a recent college graduate with a life science degree, an RN, a CRC, an international medical graduate (IMG), or even an early-career CRA navigate their experience and skills to become a successful clinical research associate? How do you chart your career path toward a six-figure income?

Many applicants fall into the trap of submitting countless resumes online without getting a single callback from Clinical Research Organizations (CROs) or pharmaceutical companies. When you do receive that coveted callback, you may not be prepared to transform that opportunity into a job offer.

This book will show you the necessary steps to become the candidate employers seek – someone who demonstrates strong work ethic, enthusiasm, superior knowledge, expertise, and ability to execute effectively. You will learn how to acquire the essential experiences needed to become a CRA, whether you've just graduated with a science degree, are a foreign-trained medical professional, or are transitioning from another role such as CRC, laboratory work, or biotechnology.

Creating a CRA-specific resume can be challenging. Without incorporating the relevant keywords, skills, and experiences, your application is unlikely to progress.

Do you know how many interview rounds to expect in today's hiring process? Are you familiar with current interview questions and optimal response strategies, including for virtual interviews that have become increasingly common?

While no resource has all the answers, this book provides a comprehensive roadmap to secure your future in clinical research. The first section introduces essential knowledge for aspiring CRAs, while the second part addresses the application process – structuring your resume, preparing for phone, video, and face-to-face interviews, anticipating interviewer questions, and asking engaging questions that demonstrate your interest and knowledge.

Before responding to another CRA job posting, consider this book essential reading. Your career trajectory is in your hands, and only you can ensure your professional goals are realized. As you proceed, keep these principles in mind:

Embrace opportunities – When opportunities present themselves, seize them promptly. If you hesitate, someone else will capitalize on them, and similar chances may not reappear. While pursuing a clinical research career, connect with a mentor or adviser, preferably an active CRA. Their industry insights, combined with the strategies from this book, will accelerate your path toward a six-figure income.

Trust your capabilities – Develop self-confidence and believe in your ability to overcome challenges. The best way to build this confidence is through comprehensive knowledge that exceeds basic requirements. This depth will make you appear knowledgeable and instill confidence in your abilities.

Act now – The clinical research industry continues to grow, with increasing demand for qualified professionals. With decentralized trials and remote monitoring becoming more common, geographic limitations have diminished, creating even more opportunities. Once you've determined clinical research is right for you, act decisively. The demand for skilled monitors remains strong, allowing you to establish a rewarding career.

The reality is that entry-level CRA positions still require relevant experience. As a life science degree holder, PhD, RN, BS graduate, pharmacist, MD, or clinical research coordinator, you already possess the foundational background to succeed as a clinical research associate. Your task now is to effectively communicate that value proposition to recruiters. This book provides the complete pathway to achieve that goal.

CHAPTER 2
WHO IS A CRA?

*P*ros are people who do jobs well even when they don't feel like it.

- Unknown Source

A Clinical Research Associate's primary function is to monitor clinical trials. A clinical study or trial is financed by a sponsor, carried out by an investigator, and monitored by a CRA. The CRA ensures that the study follows established guidelines and protocols, serving as the essential point of contact between the sponsor and the investigator throughout the study's duration. While the CRA role has diversified over the years, the core responsibility remains monitoring clinical trials to ensure adherence to standard operating procedures, the agreed protocol, Good Clinical Practice (GCP), and other relevant regulatory requirements.

CRAs may work as in-house or field-based associates for contract research organizations (CROs), pharmaceutical companies, or medical device companies—or as independent contractors. Field-based CRAs regularly visit their assigned sites, spending considerable time away from their home base. Most now work remotely from home offices, embodying the modern definition of the 21st-century professional.

The CRA's role naturally lends itself to contract work, and many professionals choose this path. They operate as independent contractors for CROs or pharmaceutical companies, which increasingly outsource larger portions of their drug development projects. This trend has accelerated with the adoption of decentralized clinical trial models and risk-based monitoring approaches.

THE INDIVIDUAL

To excel as a CRA, an individual must possess excellent interpersonal skills to collaborate with diverse stakeholders, maintain meticulous organization, demonstrate attention to detail, and efficiently manage multiple tasks simultaneously. Fortunately, these attributes can be developed as one gains experience in the industry and encounters various personalities and work environments.

For field-based CRAs or contractors, travel remains a significant aspect of the job, requiring comfort with spending several days per week away from home, though remote monitoring options have expanded in recent years.

THE CRA LIFESTYLE

The CRA lifestyle can be characterized as dynamic and mobile. CRAs are healthcare professionals who work in CROs, pharmaceutical companies, biotech firms, or as independent contractors. They oversee research studies and trials, ensuring participant safety and data integrity. Their primary responsibility is verifying that studies adhere to GCP guidelines and regulatory requirements.

While traditional CRA roles involved extensive travel (often 50-70% of working time), the industry has evolved since the COVID-19 pandemic to incorporate more remote monitoring options. Today's CRAs may have more flexible arrangements, with many organizations implementing hybrid monitoring models that combine on-site visits with remote monitoring activities.

For field-based positions, CRAs quickly adapt to life on the move— navigating different airports weekly, staying in hotels, dining out, using rental cars and rideshares at the sponsor's expense. Since CRAs typically manage multiple trials simultaneously, scheduling can be demanding even with increased remote options.

Monitoring activities generally begin around 8:30 AM and conclude by 4:30 PM, though schedules may vary based on site availability and travel requirements. CRAs often strategically plan their departure times to avoid rush hour traffic, particularly when catching flights on their final monitoring day.

The modern CRA benefits from technological advances that enable remote monitoring, risk-based approaches, and electronic data verification, providing more flexibility while maintaining the core function of ensuring trial integrity and patient safety.

CHAPTER 3
MONETARY REWARDS – THE CRA'S SALARY

t's not your salary that makes you rich; it's your spending habits.

- Charles A. Jaffe

Financial compensation is a crucial consideration when pursuing a new job or changing careers. Discussing compensation shouldn't be approached with hesitation. Inadequate research or undervaluing yourself can have lasting financial consequences.

The strongest predictors of earnings are typically education level and job experience. For CRAs, experience remains the most valuable currency. Most CROs and sponsors prefer candidates with at least a Bachelor of Science degree in life sciences. BSN nursing continues to provide a solid entry pathway, while foreign-trained physicians and pharmacists increasingly transition into clinical research monitoring roles.

For clarity, we'll examine salary structures across career levels: CRA I, CRA II, CRA III/Senior CRA, and positions exceeding $100,000 annually.

CRA I

This entry-level position typically requires 0-2 years of CRA experience. As of 2025, salary ranges for this position have increased significantly to $65,000-$85,000 annually. Candidates should possess a bachelor's degree in life sciences and some experience in clinical research, related medical/clinical experience, or research training. They should demonstrate basic knowledge of clinical research practices and regulations, including GCP guidelines and applicable regulatory frameworks.

CRA I responsibilities include conducting monitoring activities such as pre-study visits, initiation visits, routine monitoring visits, and closeout visits. They typically work under the supervision of a manager or project leader and may participate in remote monitoring activities alongside in-person site visits.

CRA II

A CRA II generally has 2-4 years of experience. Current salary ranges have increased to $75,000-$95,000 annually. While performing similar duties to a CRA I, they take on expanded responsibilities, often including supervisory elements or leadership on specific projects. Some CRA IIs hold advanced degrees (MD, PhD) in addition to meeting basic requirements. They may also lead or participate in specialized monitoring approaches like risk-based monitoring initiatives.

CRA III OR SENIOR CRA

This level requires 4-10 years of CRA experience. Compensation has grown to $90,000-$115,000 annually. Senior CRAs typically work independently, reporting to a manager or director while possessing the practical expertise to handle virtually any aspect of clinical trial monitoring. They serve as valuable resources for other CRAs and often participate in mentoring or training new hires. Many Senior CRAs specialize in complex therapeutic areas or advanced monitoring methodologies.

$100,000+ CRA POSITIONS

The clinical research career pathway definitively leads to six-figure salaries. Strategic career planning becomes increasingly important as you advance. Hands-on CRA experience remains fundamental to growth, while advanced degrees (MBA, MS, PhD, PharmD, etc.) accelerate progression toward higher compensation.

Six-figure positions are now attainable within 3-5 years in the current market, especially when strategically negotiating compensation as responsibilities increase. Management pathways such as Clinical Trial Manager, Associate Director or Director of Clinical Operations, and Vice President of Clinical Research typically command salaries well above $100,000.

The rise of specialized CRA roles has created additional pathways to premium compensation, including:

- Therapeutic area specialists (oncology, rare disease, gene therapy)
- Decentralized trial experts
- Lead CRAs with project management responsibilities
- CRAs with advanced technology platform expertise

The post-pandemic clinical research environment has increased compensation across all levels, with remote work options and signing bonuses becoming more common as organizations compete for experienced monitoring talent.

CHAPTER 4
THE CRA'S DUTIES

P
  eople tend to forget their duties but remember their rights.

- Indira Gandhi

In essence, a CRA wears many hats due to the numerous moving parts in clinical research. While monitoring remains the CRA's primary responsibility, familiarity with other aspects of clinical studies significantly enhances effectiveness. This comprehensive understanding helps connect the dots when studies deviate from planned protocols. The modern CRA's duties have evolved to include:

- Participate in budget development for trials
- Conduct pre-study visits, both on-site and virtual assessments
- Perform site initiation and monitoring visits
- Evaluate and select Principal Investigators (PIs) and sites
- Contribute to protocol development
- Conduct project feasibility assessments
- Develop or review electronic Case Report Forms (eCRFs) for clinical trials

- Resolve data queries with study site personnel
- Develop and submit documents to meet Good Clinical Practices (GCP) guidelines and SOPs
- Monitor sites to ensure compliance with clinical trial guidelines using both on-site and remote monitoring approaches
- Communicate with Principal Investigators and Trial Sponsors
- Assist in drafting clinical study reports
- Train site personnel on protocol and system requirements
- Account for investigational devices and ensure proper handling
- Verify timely collection of essential study documentation
- Maintain accurate inventory and safe storage of investigational products
- Ensure site regulatory documentation is complete and current
- Serve as a mentor to junior staff
- Lead new projects and initiatives
- Implement risk-based monitoring approaches
- Utilize electronic trial management systems and remote monitoring platforms
- Assess site data quality through centralized monitoring techniques
- Navigate decentralized and hybrid trial models

CRAs may specialize in drug trials, medical device trials, or biologics, with duties spanning numerous aspects of clinical studies. These include conducting site visits (both virtual and in-person), ensuring protocol adherence, and verifying ethical informed consent processes. They collaborate closely with study sponsors, investigators, and coordinators to maintain study integrity and progress.

The modern CRA must possess a solid understanding of GCPs and demonstrate knowledge of applicable regulations, including Title 21 of the Code of Federal Regulations in the United States, as well as ICH guidelines and regional requirements like GDPR in Europe. While traditionally requiring a life sciences degree, the field now welcomes diverse science professionals who bring valuable expertise to the clinical research environment.

As clinical trials become increasingly complex and technology-driven, today's CRA must adapt to new monitoring methodologies, electronic systems, and evolving regulatory frameworks while maintaining the fundamental commitment to patient safety and data integrity.

CHAPTER 5
HISTORY - GCPS AND REGULATIONS IN CLINICAL RESEARCH MONITORING

O*ur greatest glory is not in never falling, but in rising every time we fall.*

- Confucius

The conduct of clinical research studies and the treatment of subjects have evolved significantly over the years. This evolution includes the development of ethical standards that were absent in earlier periods. Below are the landmark developments that have shaped today's governing principles for clinical trials, which prioritize the protection of research participants.

THE NUREMBERG CODE (1947)

Following World War II and the Nuremberg Trials, the Nuremberg Code established foundational ethical principles for human experimentation. The 10 points of the Nuremberg Code remain relevant today:

1. The voluntary consent of the human subject is absolutely essential.
2. The experiment should yield fruitful results for society's benefit, be unprocurable by other methods, and not be random or unnecessary.
3. The experiment should be designed based on animal experimentation and knowledge of the disease or problem, with anticipated results justifying the experiment.
4. The experiment should avoid all unnecessary physical and mental suffering and injury.
5. No experiment should proceed where there is reason to believe death or disabling injury will occur (except when experimental physicians also serve as subjects).
6. The degree of risk should never exceed the humanitarian importance of the problem to be solved.
7. Proper preparations and facilities must protect subjects against even remote possibilities of injury, disability, or death.
8. The experiment should be conducted only by scientifically qualified persons.
9. Human subjects should be free to end the experiment if continuation seems impossible to them.
10. Scientists in charge must be prepared to terminate the experiment at any stage.

DECLARATION OF HELSINKI (1964)

This cornerstone document of human research ethics provides principles for experiments involving humans, developed by the World Medical Association. Its significance lies in being the first meaningful self-regulatory effort by the medical community in research. Initially adopted in June 1964, the Helsinki Declaration has undergone multiple revisions, most recently in 2013, with clarifying notes added in 2002, 2004, 2008, and 2013 to address emerging ethical challenges in global research.

BELMONT REPORT ETHICAL PRINCIPLES (1979)

In 1974, the United States Congress passed The National Research Act, creating the National Commission for the Protection of Human Subjects of Biomedical and Behavioral Research, which produced the Belmont Report. The report establishes three fundamental principles:

Respect for Persons – Researchers must be truthful and not deceptive. Study participants must be treated with courtesy and respect, with their autonomy protected through informed consent processes.

Beneficence – Summarized as "do no harm," this principle requires maximizing research benefits while minimizing risks to participants.

Justice – No group should be exploited for research purposes. Subject recruitment must be fair, with appropriate inclusion and exclusion criteria applied consistently.

ICH GOOD CLINICAL PRACTICES (1996/1997)

GCPs are international quality standards for clinical trial conduct, design, monitoring, auditing, recording, analysis, and reporting developed by the International Conference of Harmonization (ICH). These standards provide assurance that collected data and reported results are accurate while respecting subjects' rights, integrity, and confidentiality.

The 13 Principles of ICH GCP:

1. Trials should adhere to ethical principles.
2. Benefits, risks, and alternative procedures must be evaluated before trial initiation.
3. Research subjects' rights, safety, and welfare must take precedence.
4. Strong clinical and non-clinical data must support the trial.
5. Informed consent documentation must be established before any trial procedures.
6. IRB (Institutional Review Board) and IEC (Independent Ethics Committee) approvals must precede trial initiation.

7. Medical care and decisions must be delivered by qualified licensed physicians.
8. The Principal Investigator and medical staff must be qualified through appropriate training, education, and experience.
9. Participants must freely provide informed consent before trial participation.
10. Data must be accurately reported, interpreted, and verified to maintain quality and integrity.
11. Subjects' medical records confidentiality must be maintained.
12. The Investigational Product (IP) is the investigator's responsibility and must comply with Good Manufacturing Practice (GMP).
13. Quality control and quality assurance systems must ensure trial integrity.

Note: ICH GCP E6(R2) was implemented in 2017, adding risk-based approaches to monitoring. E6(R3) is currently being developed with further emphasis on quality-by-design principles and decentralized trial elements.

FDA CLINICAL TRIAL REGULATIONS

As a CRA, understanding how the FDA implements GCPs and U.S. regulations is essential. You must be familiar with the key sections of the Code of Federal Regulations related to clinical studies:

- **21 CFR Part 11** – Electronic Records and Signatures
- **21 CFR Part 50** – Protection of Human Subjects
- **21 CFR Part 54** – Financial Disclosure by Clinical Investigators
- **21 CFR Part 56** – Institutional Review Boards
- **21 CFR Part 312** – Investigational New Drug Application
- **21 CFR Part 314** – Applications for FDA Approval to Market a New Drug

- **21 CFR Part 11, Subpart C** – Electronic Signatures (added in 2020)
- **21 CFR Part 812** – Investigational Device Exemptions

Additionally, CRAs should be aware of global regulatory developments, including:

- **EU Clinical Trials Regulation (536/2014)** – Implemented in January 2022, replacing the previous EU Clinical Trials Directive
- **General Data Protection Regulation (GDPR)** – Affecting data privacy for EU citizens in clinical trials
- **MHRA Regulations** – Post-Brexit UK regulations for clinical trials

These regulations continue to evolve as clinical research adopts new technologies and methodologies, including decentralized clinical trials, artificial intelligence applications, and advanced data analytics.

CHAPTER 6
MUST KNOW FOR AN INTERVIEW

An investment in knowledge pays the best interest.

• Benjamin Franklin

In every clinical research process, participant safety comes first. The primary mechanisms for ensuring this safety are through Institutional Review Boards (IRBs) and the informed consent process.

INSTITUTIONAL REVIEW BOARD (IRB)

An IRB is an independent committee composed of scientific, medical, and non-scientific members whose primary mission is to protect the rights, well-being, and safety of research participants. This diverse group has ongoing responsibilities both before and throughout a clinical trial. They continuously review trials, protocols, amendments, and the methods used to obtain and document informed consent from trial participants.

Two main types of IRBs exist:

1. Institution-affiliated IRBs (connected to hospitals, universities, etc.)
2. Independent IRBs (not affiliated with an institution)

With the implementation of the revised Common Rule in 2019, single IRB (sIRB) review has become mandatory for most federally funded multi-site research in the United States, significantly changing the IRB landscape.

INFORMED CONSENT FORM (ICF)

This is the second key mechanism for maintaining the integrity and safety of human subjects in clinical trials. According to ICH GCP guidelines, informed consent is the process by which a subject voluntarily confirms willingness to participate in a particular trial after being informed of all relevant aspects. Informed consent is documented through a written, signed, and dated form.

Who approves it?

The IRB approves the ICF, and only the current approved version may be used for the project. When obtaining and documenting informed consent, the Principal Investigator must follow GCP guidelines, ethical principles, and applicable regulatory requirements. The ICF must be signed by the participant or their legally authorized representative, with a copy provided to them.

The language used in the ICF should be non-technical, straightforward, and understandable to the average person (typically at an 8th-grade reading level). Participants have the right to ask questions and must be satisfied with the answers before making a decision. They must never be coerced.

When is it obtained?

Informed consent must be obtained before any study procedures begin. When protocol amendments or new safety information becomes available, this information must be communicated to participants as soon as possible, often requiring re-consent with updated documentation.

The modern informed consent process may include electronic

consent (eConsent) options and multimedia tools to enhance participant understanding. Regardless of format, documentation of the process remains essential.

ADVERSE EVENTS (AE)

An adverse event is any unfavorable or unintended sign, symptom, or disease that occurs in a research participant after receiving an investigational product, regardless of whether it has a causal relationship to the treatment.

The study protocol specifies the definition of what constitutes an AE and how they should be reported. The investigator plays a crucial role in determining AE classification, including whether certain abnormal laboratory findings should be considered AEs.

SERIOUS ADVERSE EVENTS (SAE)

Serious Adverse Events are adverse events that result in significant medical consequences. An AE becomes an SAE when it:

- Is life-threatening
- Results in death
- Requires or prolongs hospitalization
- Causes persistent or significant disability/incapacity
- Results in congenital anomaly/birth defect
- Is another medically important condition (as defined in the protocol)

A helpful mnemonic to remember what constitutes an SAE is "CHILD":

- **C** – Congenital anomalies/Birth defects
- **H** – Hospitalization (inpatient or prolongation of existing stay)
- **I** – Incapacitation/Disability (substantial disruption of life functions)

- **L** – Life-threatening
- **D** – Death

REPORTING PROTOCOL

Sites are responsible for reporting any SAE within 24 hours of identification—by phone, fax, email, or through electronic data capture systems. The CRA must ensure this occurs promptly upon becoming aware of the event. The CRA should review the report and ensure proper medical assessment of the event before notifying the study sponsor.

INVESTIGATOR AND SPONSOR RESPONSIBILITIES

Investigators must maintain accurate records of all SAEs occurring during the trial, including time and date of occurrence, duration, and severity. They must also assess causality relationship to the investigational product.

The sponsor must be notified within 24 hours, and the IRB is informed according to local reporting requirements.

In multi-site studies, sponsors must review safety data from all sites and keep all investigators informed about SAEs across the study. The sponsor is responsible for reporting serious and unexpected adverse drug reactions to regulatory authorities within specified timeframes (e.g., 7 or 15 days depending on severity and unexpectedness).

Modern pharmacovigilance practices now include aggregate safety analysis and risk management planning throughout the product lifecycle, with increased focus on real-time safety signal detection through centralized monitoring approaches.

CHAPTER 7
CLINICAL TRIALS

A ll truths are easy to understand, once they are discovered; the point is to discover them.

• Galileo Galilei

Clinical trials are systematic studies conducted in humans to determine the safety and efficacy of new medical interventions. These trials only begin after pre-clinical testing has demonstrated sufficient safety to warrant human exposure. The clinical development process follows a carefully structured pathway divided into distinct phases.

PRE-CLINICAL TRIAL

Pre-clinical studies test new compounds in laboratory and animal models. These studies aim to collect data on acute toxicity, pharmacokinetics, metabolism, and organ sensitivity. This stage does not involve human subjects but is essential for establishing a safety profile before human exposure. Modern pre-clinical work increasingly incorporates advanced techniques like organoids, biomarkers, and computational modeling to better predict human responses.

INVESTIGATIONAL NEW DRUG (IND)

An IND is the FDA designation for experimental drugs not yet approved for marketing in the United States but permitted to be transported across state lines for clinical trials. After completing pre-clinical work demonstrating reasonable safety, drug developers submit an IND application to the FDA. This comprehensive application includes manufacturing information, pre-clinical data, clinical protocols, and investigator information. The FDA has 30 days to review the application before clinical trials may begin, provided there are no safety concerns.

CLINICAL TRIAL PHASES

Phase I Trials

Phase I studies evaluate safety in humans following pre-clinical research. Key characteristics include:

- Enrollment of a small number of participants (20-100)
- Usually conducted in healthy volunteers (except in oncology and some other serious diseases)
- Primary focus on safety, tolerability, and pharmacokinetics
- Determination of maximum tolerated dose (MTD)
- Assessment of adverse effects at different doses
- Evaluation of pharmacologic action
- In oncology and other serious conditions, patients with target diseases may participate
- May include innovative adaptive designs to accelerate development

Phase II Trials

Phase II trials follow successful Phase I studies to evaluate efficacy while continuing safety assessment. Key characteristics include:

- Enrollment of a homogeneous population (typically 100-300 participants)

- Well-controlled study design
- Participation of subjects with the target disease
- Often double-blinded with placebo, comparator drug, or both
- Primary focus on efficacy signals
- Continued monitoring of safety parameters
- May include biomarker assessments to identify responder populations
- Increasingly incorporating surrogate endpoints in certain therapeutic areas

Phase III Trials

Phase III studies compare new interventions to standard treatments or placebo to confirm efficacy and monitor side effects. Key features include:

- Large-scale enrollment (often 1,000-3,000 participants)
- Initiated only after satisfactory Phase I and II safety profiles
- Requires sufficient evidence of efficacy from earlier phases
- May continue for several years to gather comprehensive data
- Often involves multiple research centers using standardized protocols
- Data pooled across sites for analysis
- Provides the primary evidence for marketing approval
- May include diverse populations to ensure generalizability
- Often incorporates patient-reported outcomes and quality-of-life measures

Phase IV Trials

Phase IV studies occur after FDA approval and market release. Key characteristics include:

- Enrollment of several thousand participants
- Post-marketing surveillance to detect rare adverse events
- Comparison with similar products in real-world settings
- Assessment of long-term safety and effectiveness

- Familiarization of healthcare providers with new treatments
- Exploration of additional indications or patient populations
- Real-world evidence generation through registry studies and observational research
- Pharmacoeconomic analyses to demonstrate value

PRINCIPAL INVESTIGATOR (PI)

The ICH defines a PI as the individual responsible for conducting a clinical trial at a specific research site. When a study is conducted by a team, the investigator remains accountable for the entire team and assumes full responsibility for successes and shortcomings.

The PI's role encompasses securing funding, conducting the study according to protocol and regulatory requirements, and publishing results. Today's PIs must also navigate complex regulatory environments, oversee electronic data capture systems, and manage increasingly sophisticated trial designs.

FDA FORM 1572

The FDA Form 1572 (Statement of Investigator Form) must be completed and signed by the investigator and submitted to the sponsor before study initiation. The sponsor then forwards this signed form to the FDA. CRAs must verify that the current version of Form 1572 is being used.

An investigator completes Form 1572 for two primary reasons:

1. To document for the sponsor that the investigator possesses the necessary qualifications and experience, and that the site has adequate facilities to support the trial
2. To inform the investigator of their obligations and commitments to the study

Once signed, Form 1572 becomes a legally binding document, committing the investigator to conduct the study in accordance with regulations and requirements specified in the form.

Must the Investigator be a physician?

According to 21 CFR 312.53(a), sponsors must select individuals qualified by training and experience, but investigators are not required to be physicians. However, if a non-physician serves as the investigator, a physician must be included as a sub-investigator to handle all medical decisions related to the trial.

Investigator responsibilities include:

- Supervising or conducting the trial according to protocol
- Ensuring all subjects complete informed consent documentation
- Complying with regulations and protocol requirements
- Being thoroughly familiar with the Investigator Brochure before trial initiation
- Managing and reporting adverse events appropriately
- Maintaining accurate and complete study records
- Accounting for investigational product
- Ensuring adequate resources to conduct the study

Modern investigator responsibilities have expanded to include oversight of electronic systems, implementing risk-based approaches, and managing increasingly complex protocol designs in today's evolving clinical research environment.

FDA Form 1572

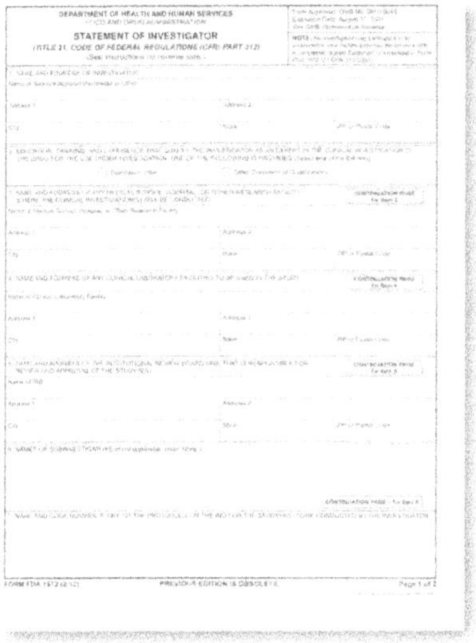

DEPARTMENT OF HEALTH AND HUMAN SERVICES

FOOD AND DRUG ADMINISTRATION

STATEMENT OF INVESTIGATOR

(TITLE 21, CODE OF FEDERAL REGULATIONS (CFR) PART 312)

FORM FDA 1572 PREVIOUS EDITION IS OBSOLETE Page 1 of 2

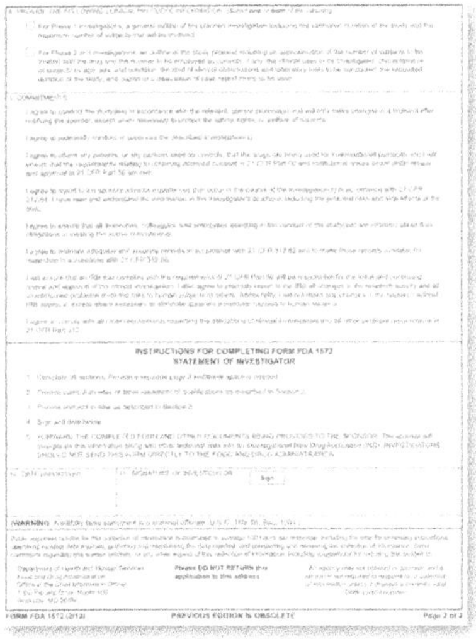

INSTRUCTIONS FOR COMPLETING FORM FDA 1572

STATEMENT OF INVESTIGATOR

FORM FDA 1572 PREVIOUS EDITION IS OBSOLETE Page 2 of 2

CHAPTER 8
AUDITS

W*here there is shouting, there is no true knowledge.*

- Leonardo da Vinci

An audit, as defined by ICH, is a systematic and independent examination of trial-related documents to authenticate that trial-related activities were carried out and data was collected, analyzed, recorded, and accurately reported in accordance with GCPs, sponsors' SOPs, and the study protocol.

SPONSOR AUDITS

Sponsor audits serve two primary purposes: to ensure site compliance with study protocols and applicable regulations in preparation for potential regulatory inspections, and to verify that the study is progressing according to plan or to investigate suspected protocol or regulatory deviations.

Types of Sponsor Audits

Routine Audits – These proactive assessments are conducted by sponsors to verify site compliance with regulations and protocol requirements. Any identified issues are addressed to ensure readiness for potential regulatory inspections. Routine audits may be scheduled based on risk assessment, enrollment metrics, or as part of standard quality oversight.

For-Cause Audits – These more targeted investigations are typically initiated when a CRA or other monitoring activities report compliance issues at a site. For-cause audits focus on specific concerns and may require more extensive documentation review and corrective action planning.

Modern sponsor audits increasingly incorporate:

- Remote audit components using secure electronic systems
- Risk-based approaches focusing on critical data and processes
- Real-time data analytics to identify potential issues proactively
- Specialized expertise for complex therapeutic areas and technologies

FDA AUDITS

The FDA conducts inspections or audits of investigative sites to verify study conduct and data integrity. These regulatory inspections focus on two key areas:

1. **Data Integrity** – Ensuring the quality and integrity of data submitted to the FDA is accurate and properly maintained. This includes verifying that data was collected under appropriate conditions and that all information is valid and traceable. FDA inspectors review source documentation, case report forms, essential documents, and data management practices.
2. **Protection of Human Research Subjects** – Evaluating how research participants were treated by all parties involved in the trial, including the CRO, sponsor, investigative site, and PI. Inspectors verify adherence to guidelines, GCPs,

regulations, and the approved protocol, with particular focus on ensuring that participant safety, rights, and welfare remained top priorities throughout the study.

The FDA has expanded its inspection approach to include:

- Bioresearch Monitoring (BIMO) program focusing on clinical investigators, sponsors, IRBs, and nonclinical laboratories
- Risk-based site selection for inspections
- Increased attention to electronic systems and data integrity
- International inspection coordination with other regulatory authorities
- Greater focus on sponsor oversight of CROs and sites

Other regulatory authorities, including the European Medicines Agency (EMA), Health Canada, and Japan's PMDA, also conduct inspections following similar principles with region-specific requirements.

CRAs play a critical role in ensuring sites are inspection-ready by maintaining comprehensive documentation, addressing issues promptly, and fostering a culture of quality and compliance throughout the clinical trial process.

CHAPTER 9
CLINICAL RESEARCH MONITORING VISITS

N *othing in life is to be feared, it is only to be understood. Now is the time to understand more, so that we may fear less.*

- Marie Curie

Monitoring visits constitute the core responsibilities of a CRA. These activities ensure that clinical studies progress as expected, adhering to GCPs, current SOPs, and protocol requirements. Effective monitoring identifies and addresses concerns or problems promptly during these interactions.

The four primary types of monitoring visits conducted by CRAs include:

- Pre-study visits
- Initiation visits
- Routine monitoring visits
- Closeout visits

PRE-STUDY VISITS

Also known as site qualification visits, these assessments determine whether investigators and staff possess the necessary experience and training in the specific therapeutic area to deliver successful and credible study outcomes.

Planning for the Pre-study Visit

This process typically begins after an investigator expresses interest in a study and receives preliminary approval from the sponsor.

Before the visit, the project manager or CRA should have:

- A letter from the site investigator confirming the appointment
- An agenda outlining discussion topics
- Confirmation from the site regarding the visit

During the Visit
The CRA should:

- Verify availability of qualified and experienced personnel
- Obtain signed and dated CVs of the investigator and key staff
- Discuss the investigational product background
- Assess the site's experience with similar studies
- Ensure understanding of GCP guidelines, IRB requirements, and regulatory practices
- Confirm access to the target subject population
- Evaluate facility adequacy (examining rooms, storage, pharmacy, etc.)
- Review the proposed protocol design
- Discuss informed consent procedures
- Assess pharmacy capabilities, storage facilities, and security measures
- Evaluate electronic data capture capabilities and preferences
- Discuss enrollment targets and timelines
- Determine appropriate monitoring frequency

- Evaluate site's experience with remote or decentralized trial procedures (if applicable)
- Assess technological infrastructure for hybrid or virtual monitoring capabilities

After the Qualification Visit

The CRA prepares a study-specific qualification visit report. Once approved, this report is forwarded to the sponsor or representative, including a statement on site suitability. Additionally, a follow-up letter is sent to the investigator summarizing findings and indicating approval or rejection of the site.

INITIATION VISITS

This visit is typically conducted by the assigned CRA or another qualified person designated by the project manager. The initiation visit takes place at the study site and generally requires a full working day.

The purpose is to review study protocols, procedures, and processes to ensure all site staff understand requirements before study commencement.

Planning for an Initiation Visit

Before the visit, the CRA should:

- Send a letter confirming the initiation visit
- Schedule a mutually agreeable time
- Prepare an agenda of discussion topics
- Confirm the site's acknowledgment of the visit
- Ensure study materials and equipment have been delivered (if applicable)

During the Visit

Key site personnel should attend, including the site coordinator, data manager, pharmacy staff, and principal or sub-investigator. Sometimes the sponsor representatives also attend.

Activities include:

- Documenting all attendees
- Reviewing the study protocol in detail
- Explaining clinical trial objectives
- Addressing investigational product handling (storage, preparation, administration)
- Identifying CRA workspace
- Discussing PI responsibilities regarding protocol adherence
- Defining adverse events (AEs) and serious adverse events (SAEs)
- Identifying staff responsible for obtaining informed consent
- Reviewing informed consent procedures
- Verifying use of current IRB-approved consent forms
- Establishing processes for providing subjects with signed ICF copies
- Reviewing the regulatory binder
- Training staff on CRF/EDC completion
- Identifying source documentation required for verification
- Establishing routine monitoring visit frequency
- Training on any study-specific technology platforms
- Reviewing data privacy and security procedures
- Discussing remote and on-site monitoring expectations

After the Visit

The CRA drafts an Initiation Study Report summarizing discussions and training activities, then submits it to the project manager.

ROUTINE MONITORING VISIT (RMV)

Also called Interim Monitoring Visits, these regular assessments are conducted by the CRA. Key site personnel (investigator, coordinator, nurse) should be available. Visit frequency varies (typically monthly or bimonthly) as specified in the monitoring plan, with each visit normally lasting around 8 hours.

Planning for RMV

Two weeks before the visit, the CRA should send notification of the planned RMV, propose dates, and receive confirmation from the site.

During the Visit
The CRA will:

- Review source documents for enrolled subjects
- Verify PI and staff qualifications remain current
- Inspect pharmacy / storage areas (if applicable)
- Confirm enrolled subjects meet eligibility criteria
- Review CRFs / EDC data for completeness and accuracy
- Verify proper informed consent was obtained for new participants
- Ensure AEs and SAEs are accurately reported and communicated
- Review data queries and corrections
- Verify essential document maintenance
- Reconcile investigational product accountability
- Assess protocol compliance
- Provide ongoing training as needed
- Discuss enrollment progress
- Address any site concerns or challenges
- Evaluate remote monitoring findings (if applicable)

After the Visit

The CRA prepares a monitoring report documenting findings, actions, and recommendations, which is submitted to the project manager and filed according to sponsor requirements.

CLOSEOUT VISITS

Conducted by the monitoring CRA or another trained individual, closeout visits occur at study completion or site termination. In some circumstances, closeouts may be conducted remotely without an on-site visit.

Before the Visit

The CRA notifies the site of the planned closeout and confirms a date when the investigator and coordinator will be available.

During the Visit

Activities include:

- Documenting and verifying remaining supplies
- Confirming disposition of unused investigational products and materials
- Reviewing record retention requirements with the investigator
- Verifying all ICFs are properly signed and stored
- Ensuring all SAE forms and data corrections are complete
- Notifying the IRB of study completion
- Reconciling all outstanding data queries
- Reviewing final CRF/EDC entries for completeness
- Confirming all essential documents are present in the regulatory binder
- Discussing publication plans and future communications
- Collecting any sponsor-owned equipment
- Addressing any outstanding financial matters

After the Visit

The CRA prepares a comprehensive closeout visit report for submission to the sponsor, documenting the completion of all required activities and any outstanding issues.

The modern clinical research environment has expanded monitoring approaches to include risk-based monitoring strategies, remote monitoring capabilities, and centralized data review. Today's CRAs often employ a hybrid approach combining traditional on-site visits with virtual interactions and data analytics, especially since the COVID-19 pandemic accelerated adoption of decentralized trial elements. Regardless of methodology, the fundamental purpose remains ensuring protocol adherence, data integrity, and subject safety throughout the clinical trial process.

CHAPTER 10
FINDING A CRA JOB – WHERE TO BEGIN

R*ecession is when a neighbor loses his job. Depression is when you lose yours.*

- Ronald Reagan

Choose a job you love, and you will never have to work a day in your life.

- Confucius

Now that you have a foundational understanding of a CRA's responsibilities, we can begin the journey of creating a successful application strategy for entering this field.

GET A MENTOR

To embark on any journey, you need to know your destination and have guidance—whether a map or today's GPS equivalent. In the clinical research landscape, your mentor serves as your navigation system, helping you avoid wrong turns and identify optimal pathways.

This principle applies directly to clinical research careers. A mentor can assist you in navigating the entire process of securing a CRA position, advancing within the field, taking on greater responsibilities, and ultimately increasing your compensation.

Finding a mentor shouldn't be left to chance. Perhaps you hadn't considered needing a mentor for your job search, but having one significantly streamlines the process. They'll help you recognize opportunities you might otherwise miss and provide encouragement when challenges arise, advising whether to persist or pivot your approach. The choice is yours: find the right mentor or resign yourself to struggling through the process through trial and error.

WHOM TO CHOOSE

When selecting a mentor, consider these essential criteria:

1. **Current industry involvement** - Choose someone actively working as a CRA, not retired, who remains engaged with current practices and trends.
2. **Relevant experience** - Your mentor should have substantial clinical research experience, ideally with a similar background to yours, providing that valuable "been there, done that" perspective.
3. **Professional integrity** - Select someone whose character and professional conduct you can respect and emulate.
4. **Genuine interest** - Your mentor should demonstrate a sincere interest in your development and success.
5. **Industry connections** - Someone with a strong professional network can provide introductions and insights about opportunities.
6. **Knowledge of current hiring practices** - The clinical research landscape has evolved significantly, with remote work options, specialized therapeutic areas, and new technologies changing how companies recruit.

Begin your search within your existing network—ask family and friends if they know any CRAs who might introduce you to the field.

University career centers can often connect you with alumni working in clinical research. Professional networking platforms like LinkedIn have made identifying potential mentors easier than ever, with many industry groups and forums where you can make connections.

If your chosen mentor is a new acquaintance without prior knowledge of your capabilities, it's crucial to make a positive impression. Demonstrate enthusiasm, professionalism, and a genuine commitment to learning. Be courteous, personable, and direct in your communications. People naturally gravitate toward positive individuals, so approach interactions with cheerfulness and eagerness to learn. Seek their guidance respectfully and follow through on their recommendations.

Remember that mentorship is a two-way relationship—while you receive guidance, look for appropriate ways to express appreciation and potentially offer value in return, whether through your perspective, technical skills, or simply your commitment to making the most of their advice.

CHAPTER 11
HOW TO GET CRA EXPERIENCE

*W*hen *you are asked if you can do a job, tell 'em, "Certainly I can!" Then get busy and find out how to do it.*

- Theodore Roosevelt

When searching job sites like LinkedIn, Indeed, or Monster, you'll encounter numerous CRA positions across the country - CRA I, CRA II, Regional CRA positions, and more. However, when applying with a life science degree or relevant medical background, you may receive few or no responses.

This occurs because most "entry-level" CRA positions still require candidates with prior CRA experience or clinical research involvement. This creates a frustrating paradox: how do you gain the necessary experience when entry-level positions already demand it?

The reality is that truly experience-free CRA positions are rare. Below are effective strategies to gain relevant experience before applying for CRA roles.

PROACTIVE OUTREACH

This approach consistently yields results but requires persistence and patience. Begin by researching clinical research departments at local academic medical centers, hospitals, and research institutions. Review their ongoing studies and therapeutic areas of focus. When you identify interesting research, contact the Principal Investigator or Clinical Research Coordinator (typically listed on the website) with a tailored introduction.

For example, introduce yourself as a recent science graduate or ECFMG-certified IMG interested in their research and willing to contribute as a volunteer or in a paid capacity.

You may receive interest or be told they don't currently need assistance. Use any response as an opportunity to establish a connection - let them know they can contact you when needs arise and that you'll periodically check in. Continue this approach with multiple research groups until successful. Prepare for rejections but maintain your momentum. Remember: persistence pays off, and you'll never succeed if you don't try.

Modern outreach benefits from professional platforms like LinkedIn, where you can directly connect with research professionals and demonstrate your knowledge through meaningful engagement before making specific requests.

STRATEGIC NETWORKING

Contrary to what you might expect, many CROs don't readily accept volunteers without expecting something in return. Finding volunteer opportunities requires strategic networking.

This approach may require maintaining another job while volunteering part-time. Start by connecting with people already working as CRAs who can advocate for you to their colleagues. Industry associations, clinical research meetups (both virtual and in-person), and relevant LinkedIn groups can also provide valuable connections.

Once you secure a position, maximize your learning opportunities within the time available. Demonstrate exceptional work ethic and build positive relationships without overstepping boundaries. These connections may offer you positions when they become available or provide strong references for future applications.

Today's networking opportunities have expanded with virtual industry events, webinars, and online communities focused on clinical research, offering additional pathways to make connections while demonstrating your knowledge.

CRA TRAINING PROGRAMS

Formal CRA training through online or in-person programs provides valuable foundational knowledge. While these programs typically cost several hundred dollars, they're worthwhile investments, especially for those with science degrees but no clinical research experience.

These programs teach clinical research monitoring fundamentals while offering opportunities to connect with industry professionals and those affiliated with CROs, pharmaceutical companies, and experienced CRAs.

Before enrolling, negotiate assistance with job placement or professional references. Inquire about opportunities for hands-on experience with research studies, and get these commitments in writing before payment.

After enrollment, proactively ensure the program delivers on its promises. Seize opportunities as they arise, and leverage program instructors' knowledge about specific employers and their hiring practices.

Industry-recognized programs with strong placement records have become increasingly valuable as companies look for candidates with standardized training foundations.

ONLINE TRAINING AND CERTIFICATIONS

Organizations like the National Institutes of Health, SOCRA, ACRP, and various government entities offer free or affordable online courses covering different aspects of clinical research. These self-paced programs typically require several hours to complete.

After finishing courses and passing assessments, you'll gain solid foundational knowledge and receive certificates that strengthen your resume and demonstrate commitment during interviews. The "Resume Building" section will show you how to effectively highlight these qualifications.

Remember that most organizations provide training to new CRAs, but they prefer candidates with some understanding of the field. Typical onboarding includes overview of regulations and guidelines for clinical research and human subject protection, followed by organization-specific monitoring procedures to ensure data integrity and GCP compliance.

Valuable online training resources include:

- http://www.nihtraining.com/
- CITI Program (https://about.citiprogram.org/)
- ACRP eLearning
- TransCelerate Biopharma's GCP training
- Clinical Research Society programs
- LinkedIn Learning clinical research courses

Modern CRA roles increasingly require familiarity with electronic data capture systems, remote monitoring practices, and risk-based approaches. Targeted training in these areas can further differentiate your application in today's evolving clinical research environment.

CHAPTER 12
CERTIFICATION – DO YOU NEED IT?

never let schooling interfere with my education.

• Mark Twain

While many training institutions provide certificates upon completion of formal CRA training programs (excluding degree-granting universities), these credentials don't necessarily carry significant weight across the industry.

In the United States, two organizations offer certifications that receive widespread recognition within the clinical research industry: ACRP (Association of Clinical Research Professionals) and SOCRA (Society of Clinical Research Associates). Certifications from these organizations are well-respected and acknowledged throughout the sector.

However, these industry-recognized certifications typically serve as career enhancement tools after you've accumulated several years of CRA experience. They help advance your clinical research career once you're already established in the field. When applying for entry-level positions or without prior clinical research experience, your resources and energy are better invested in gaining practical experience or completing a formal CRA training program.

Currently, employers don't place excessive emphasis on ACRP or SOCRA certifications. However, the landscape is evolving, and these credentials may become more important or even required in the future. This pattern has occurred in other healthcare fields—for example, pharmacy technician certification was once optional with employers focusing primarily on experience. Now, without this certification, candidates cannot even begin discussions with potential employers.

If you're already working as a CRA or CRC with several years of experience, investigating these certification options may be worthwhile to ensure you're well-positioned for future requirements. By obtaining certification proactively, you'll stay ahead of potential industry shifts if certification becomes mandatory for all CRAs.

The certification landscape has continued to evolve since this book was first published. Additional credentials that have gained recognition include:

- CCRA (Certified Clinical Research Associate) through ACRP
- CCRP (Certified Clinical Research Professional) through SOCRA
- ICH GCP Investigator certification
- Specialized certifications in areas like oncology research or data management

Many organizations now offer tiered certification programs that accommodate professionals at different career stages, including those with limited experience who previously couldn't qualify. Some pharmaceutical companies and CROs have also developed their own credentialing programs to standardize training across their organizations.

While certification remains optional for entry-level positions, the increasing complexity of clinical trials and growing emphasis on quality standards suggests that formal credentials may play a more significant role in career advancement in the coming years.

CHAPTER 13
HOW TO PUT YOUR CRA RESUME TOGETHER

"Talent is only the starting point."

- Irving Berlin

Your resume determines whether you'll receive an interview invitation, making its content critically important. For this discussion, we'll assume you're a life science degree holder, registered nurse, or international medical graduate with legal work authorization in the United States.

With technological advances, the competition to get your resume noticed by the right reviewers has intensified. Recruiters typically review numerous resumes daily and have developed specific screening criteria or utilize applicant tracking systems (ATS) for initial filtering.

HOW TO GET YOUR RESUME IN FRONT OF THE RIGHT PEOPLE

Organizations either outsource resume screening to third parties or employ internal HR departments for this function. Most use software that scans resumes for specific keywords relevant to the job description. Understanding this process is essential for creating an effective resume.

Modern applicant tracking systems have become increasingly sophisticated, analyzing not only keywords but also contextual relevance, experience duration, and even the placement of information within your document. To maximize visibility:

- Research industry-specific terminology and incorporate relevant keywords naturally throughout your resume
- Tailor your document to match specific job descriptions
- Use standard section headings that ATS software can easily recognize
- Submit in recommended file formats (typically .docx or .pdf)

RESUME LAYOUT

The visual organization of your resume significantly impacts its effectiveness. With recruiters reviewing dozens or hundreds of resumes daily, creating a document that highlights pertinent information increases your chances of securing an interview.

Keep your resume clean, professional, and easily scannable. Remember that no single resume template works for every situation—each document should be customized for the specific position. Ensure you thoroughly understand every detail on your resume and can elaborate on each element of your education, experience, and activities during interviews.

When developing your resume, follow these guidelines to create a compelling document while avoiding common pitfalls:

- Highlight your strengths prominently
- Eliminate clutter by removing irrelevant experiences, unless they fill chronological gaps that might otherwise raise questions
- Place your name prominently at the top of the document without a separate "Resume" heading

- Use powerful action verbs throughout to convey accomplishment and initiative
- Present job experiences in reverse chronological order (most recent first)
- Be prepared to explain any gaps with specific, honest responses

For clinical research positions, emphasize your understanding of regulatory requirements, experience with clinical trial procedures, knowledge of GCP guidelines, and any relevant therapeutic area expertise. Even without direct CRA experience, highlight transferable skills such as attention to detail, communication abilities, organizational capabilities, and analytical thinking that make you well-suited for monitoring responsibilities.

Action Words
acted
adapted
developed
interviewed
reviewed
devised
introduced
revitalized
addressed
diagnosed
invented
scheduled
administered
directed
investigated
screened
advised
dispatched
lectured
allocated
drafted

maintained
analyzed
edited
appraised
enabled
approved
encouraged
mediated
arbitrated
engineered
moderated
arranged
enlisted
monitored
assembled
established
motivated
managed
marketed
set goals
shaped
solved
specified
spoke
stimulated
strengthened
summarized
assigned
evaluated
negotiated
supervised
attained
examined
operated
audited
executed

organized
authored
explained
originated
balanced
extracted
overhauled
budgeted
fabricated
oversaw
built
facilitated
performed
surveyed
systematized
tabulated
trained
translated
calculated
fashioned
persuaded
upgraded
catalogued
forecasted
planned
validated
chaired
formulated
prepared
wrote
clarified
founded
prioritized
classified
generated
processed

coached
guided
produced
collected
identified
programmed
communicated
illustrated
projected
compiled
implemented
promoted
computed
improved
publicized
conceptualized
increased
purchased
consolidated
influenced
contracted
informed
recommended
reconciled
coordinated
initiated
recorded
corresponded
inspected
recruited
created
instituted
critiqued
instructed
delegated
integrated

designed
interpreted
remodeled
repair
researched
retrieved

There are different ways to lay out your resume, but we have found the layout below to be very effective (Note: Your name and address line must be centered):

NAME Street Address, City, State, Zip Code | Phone Number | Email Address

OBJECTIVE A clear, concise statement about the position you're seeking and how your skills align with it. For CRA positions, specifically mention clinical research monitoring and your interest in ensuring study integrity and compliance.

EDUCATION List your degrees in reverse chronological order (most recent first) Degree, Institution, Location, Graduation Date

- Include relevant coursework, projects, or research experience
- List GPA if it's strong (3.5 or above)

CERTIFICATIONS/TRAINING

- Clinical Research-Related Certifications (NIH Human Subjects Protection, GCP Training, etc.)
- Therapeutic Area-Specific Training (if applicable)
- Technical Skills (EDC systems, MS Office, etc.)

RELEVANT EXPERIENCE Position Title, Company/Institution, Location, Dates

- Use bullet points with action verbs to describe responsibilities and achievements
- Quantify results whenever possible

- Highlight experience related to clinical research, monitoring, or transferable skills
- Focus on compliance, documentation, quality control, and relationship management

OTHER EXPERIENCE Position Title, Company/Institution, Location, Dates

- Include relevant transferable skills from positions outside clinical research
- Focus on skills applicable to CRA responsibilities: attention to detail, time management, etc.

SKILLS

- Technical Skills: List specific systems, software, or methodologies relevant to clinical research
- Language Skills: Note any additional languages you speak (important for global studies)
- Interpersonal Skills: Communication, problem-solving, time management

PROFESSIONAL MEMBERSHIPS

- Relevant clinical research organizations (ACRP, SOCRA, etc.)
- Industry-specific associations related to your therapeutic background

REFERENCES "Available upon request" (or omit this section completely as it's generally understood)

JOB-SPECIFIC RESUMES

After creating your basic CRA resume, customize it for each specific position you apply for. Save these tailored versions on your computer using file names that include the company name to avoid confusion as you apply to different organizations.

The key is to adapt each resume to the advertised position. Generic resumes are no longer effective in today's competitive job market. Fortunately, once you've developed a solid base resume, most of your work is done—it will serve as a template requiring only minor customizations for specific opportunities.

Carefully analyze each job posting, noting required skills, responsibilities, and qualifications. Ensure all relevant keywords appear in your resume. While you'll have skills and experiences not mentioned in the advertisement, focus on matching your qualifications to their stated needs. When you find alignment between your experience and their requirements, incorporate their phrasing into your resume using your own words. Review these sections to ensure they flow naturally with the rest of your document.

This approach is crucial because initial resume screenings are often conducted by third parties or HR professionals without clinical research backgrounds. When your resume doesn't reflect the language and requirements in the job description, reviewers may quickly move to the next candidate. However, when your document contains the specific keywords and requirements they're seeking, appropriately integrated throughout your resume, you significantly increase your chances of securing an interview.

REFERENCES

After receiving a job offer, most employers request references to gain additional perspective on your qualifications and work style. They want insights from credible sources who can speak to your capabilities based on substantial interaction.

Potential employers seek references from reputable and knowledgeable individuals—typically managers or supervisors from previous employers, or professors from your educational background. These individuals can provide meaningful evaluation of your skills and work ethic.

Securing strong references requires deliberate effort. Approach people you trust who meet the appropriate criteria, and be direct in your request. Avoid indirect or ambiguous requests, as these may result in lukewarm or even negative references that could derail your application. Ask directly and gauge their response immediately.

When making your request, after appropriate pleasantries, try a straightforward approach: "I'm applying for a CRA position with XY Company, and I'm wondering if you would be comfortable providing a strong recommendation as a reference."

If you detect any hesitation or uncertainty in their response, it's best to seek references elsewhere. A lukewarm reference can be more damaging than having fewer references.

REFERENCES FROM YOUR CURRENT CRA NETWORKS

Leverage your connections with practicing CRAs to identify open positions within their organizations. When opportunities exist, send them your resume and ask them to forward it directly to human resources. This approach ensures your resume reaches the right people and benefits from internal advocacy. Many employers offer employee referral bonuses ranging from $1,000 to $5,000 for successful hiring recommendations.

To maximize their chances of earning this referral bonus, your contact has a financial interest in your success. They can provide valuable insights on how to excel during the interview process, including company-specific tips that might not be available to outside candidates. When approaching CRAs who seem reluctant to assist, gently remind them of the potential referral bonus—this financial incentive often motivates greater support for your candidacy.

The power of internal referrals has only increased in recent years, with many organizations prioritizing employee-referred candidates due to their higher retention rates and cultural fit. A strong internal advocate can make a significant difference in the competitive CRA job market.

CHAPTER 14
PREPARING FOR THE CRA INTERVIEW

f it's your job to eat a frog, it's best to do it first thing in the morning. And if it's your job to eat two frogs, it's best to eat the biggest one first.

- Mark Twain

Once your resume has been shortlisted by a CRO as a potential CRA candidate, they'll schedule an initial phone interview. You'll typically receive a call thanking you for applying and inquiring about your availability for a phone conversation lasting 30 minutes to an hour. For some candidates, this might be the only interview before receiving an offer, while for others, it represents the first in a series of interviews.

PHONE INTERVIEW

When you receive that initial call expressing interest, resist the temptation to immediately agree to a phone interview without preparation. Phone interviews are critical screening tools that can make or break your candidacy. They determine whether you advance from candidate to potential employee. A poor performance will likely prevent you from securing a face-to-face interview.

PREPARING FOR PHONE INTERVIEWS

Organizations invest carefully in their hiring process, and they want to ensure you're a promising candidate before extending an invitation for an in-person meeting. The phone screening involves a series of questions to assess your monitoring experience and overall fit. While the format resembles a face-to-face interview, the preparation you do for phone interviews will also serve you well in subsequent in-person meetings.

Second or Third Phone Interviews

Follow-up phone interviews are typically conducted by senior HR personnel or a CRA manager. As your candidacy advances to this stage, they seek more detailed information about your clinical research experience. Your responses at this level significantly influence whether you progress further in the selection process.

I strongly recommend taking detailed notes to ensure consistency in your responses across all interview stages, particularly regarding the number of visits conducted, years of experience, and similar quantifiable information. A tracking system for all relevant questions helps maintain consistency throughout the interview process.

Key information interviewers typically want to know includes:

- Your total years of monitoring experience
- Types of organizations you've worked with (medical device, pharmaceutical, or CRO)
- Clinical trial phases you've participated in (I, II, III, or IV)
- Experience with on-site or field monitoring
- Number of studies you've been involved in from pre-study visits through closeouts
- Therapeutic areas in which you've worked
- Experience with remote or hybrid monitoring approaches
- Familiarity with electronic data capture systems and risk-based monitoring
- Comfort with virtual communication tools for site interaction

13 TIPS FOR A SUCCESSFUL PHONE INTERVIEW

1. **Choose a quiet environment** free from distractions when taking the call. Ensure no children, pets, or other potential disruptions are present that could create unpleasant background noise.

2. **Use a reliable phone connection** - preferably a landline for maximum clarity. If using a cell phone, verify excellent reception beforehand. Poor sound quality can frustrate interviewers and negatively impact their perception.

3. **Prepare reference materials** in advance and have them accessible during the call. This advantage of phone interviews allows you to consult notes without the interviewer's knowledge.

4. **Organize information in bullet points** for quick reference, but deliver responses naturally to avoid sounding rehearsed or reading directly from notes.

5. **Pace your responses** thoughtfully, remembering that interviewers are likely taking notes. Allow time for them to record your answers between responses.

6. **Document your own answers** for consistency in future interviews. Create a simple tracking system to maintain uniform responses across multiple conversations.

7. **Conduct mock interviews** before the actual call. Prepare for likely questions and practice delivering concise, relevant responses.

8. **Smile while speaking** even though the interviewer can't see you. Voice experts confirm that smiling positively affects your vocal tone and energy, which interviewers can detect.

9. **Keep your resume at hand** and know it thoroughly. Have a copy in front of you during the interview for quick reference.

10. **Be prepared to walk through your background** chronologically, from education through your current or most recent position.

11. **Ensure your resume follows logical progression** so the

interviewer can easily follow your career narrative without confusion.

12. **Have explanations ready for employment gaps** that are honest, concise, and confidently delivered. Address these proactively without hesitation.

13. **Research the company thoroughly** before the interview. When asked why you're interested in the position or organization, reference specific aspects of their work that align with your experience and career goals.

Today's phone interviews may also include video components through platforms like Zoom or Teams. The same principles apply, with additional attention to professional appearance, appropriate background, and camera positioning if video is involved.

Phone Interview Work Sheet

How many years of monitoring experience do you have?

What type(s) of organization did you work for? E.g. CRO, Pharma, medical device company?

Which phases of a clinical trial have you been involved in?
Phase I...............
Phase II...............
Phase III...............
Phase IV...............

How many studies have you been involved in from pre study visit to close out visit?

Provide a range for the visits listed below which you have completed in the course of your career as a clinical research assistant:-

- Pre-study visits...............
- Initiation visits...............
- Routine monitoring visits......
- Close out visits...............

Which therapeutic area(s) have you worked in?

Therapeutic Area E.g. Oncology	1st	2nd	3rd	Years of Experience

Describe your experiences/Type of study in the therapeutic areas outlined above

Therapeutic area	Experience/Study
Oncology	Breast cancer drug trial

CHAPTER 15
DRESSING FOR THE FACE-TO-FACE INTERVIEW FOR MEN AND WOMEN

*Y*ou cannot climb the ladder of success dressed in the costume of failure.

• Zig Ziglar

Not all phone interviews lead to face-to-face meetings. In some cases, organizations may offer positions based solely on phone performance and previous experience. However, when interviews progress to in-person meetings, proper preparation becomes essential.

In face-to-face interviews, your appearance, body language, and overall demeanor significantly impact first impressions. You must look professional and appropriate for the role. Business casual is insufficient - business professional attire is required. You needn't invest in expensive clothing, but your appearance should be polished and appropriate. Ideally, interviewers should remember you rather than what you wore, indicating your attire was suitable and not distracting.

While appropriate attire may not significantly enhance your interview performance, inappropriate clothing will definitely detract from it. Starting with appropriate attire gives you a neutral foundation, while inappropriate dress immediately creates a negative impression.

FOR MEN

As a CRA, you'll represent your employer when monitoring sites. Your interview appearance gives prospective employers insight into how you'll represent them professionally. They seek candidates who project competence and professionalism.

A suit remains the standard professional outfit for men. The color choice matters significantly - stick with solid black, navy, gray, or pinstripes. Avoid bright colors or patterns that distract from your qualifications. Interviewers should remember your skills and experience, not "the guy with the yellow suit."

Expensive or trendy suits aren't necessary, but proper fit is crucial. Ill-fitting clothing that requires constant adjustment creates distractions. If a full suit isn't available, a navy blue sport jacket with matching trousers works well. Budget-conscious options are available at department stores like JC Penney or discount retailers.

The Shirt

Choose a long-sleeved shirt, particularly if you might remove your jacket. Pale blue, white, or other solid colors work best. Ensure proper sizing - the shirt should remain tucked when you raise your arms, and the collar should provide comfortable breathing room.

The Tie

Power colors include red and navy blue. Avoid ties with bright colors or novelty designs. Solid colors, subtle repeating patterns, or discreet polka dots are appropriate. If coordinating shirts and ties challenges you, consider purchasing pre-matched sets.

Shoes and Socks

Wear black or brown leather dress shoes that are clean, polished, and in good condition. Avoid sneakers and white socks - choose dark socks that match your suit color.

Grooming and Accessories

Conservative grooming is essential. Be well-groomed with neat hair. Men should avoid earrings, necklaces, and decorative rings. A wedding band is appropriate if married, but other jewelry should be minimized. Your scent should be subtle - light cologne or just deodorant is sufficient. Avoid any hint of alcohol on your breath, even if you're only a social drinker.

FOR WOMEN

The Suit

Women have more attire options, but business professional remains the standard for interviews. You'll represent your organization, so professional appearance is crucial.

A skirt suit or pantsuit in dark maroon, gray, charcoal, or black is ideal. Avoid bold colors, flashy patterns, and mini-skirts. Classic professional attire serves you better than current fashion trends, which might distract from your qualifications. The interview isn't the occasion for fashion statements.

The Blouse

Choose a complementary color to your suit - white, pastel, or cream works well. Silk or cotton fabrics without distracting embellishments are appropriate. Ensure modest necklines that don't display cleavage.

The Shoes

Select shoes that complement your suit color. Simple pumps with moderate heels are advisable. Avoid boots or extremely high heels that might distract or impede comfortable movement during the interview day, which may include facility tours.

Today's interviewing landscape has evolved to include more virtual options, but when in-person meetings occur, these professional standards remain important for clinical research positions where you'll represent your organization to investigators, site staff, and other stakeholders.

CHAPTER 16

INTERVIEW QUESTIONS TO ANTICIPATE AND HOW TO RESPOND

"*Many of life's failures are people who did not realize how close they were to success when they gave up.*"

- Thomas Edison

If you've prepared thoroughly for phone interviews, you'll be well-positioned for in-person meetings. As with phone interviews, practice through mock sessions in front of a mirror or with a friend. The foundation of successful interviewing is mastering your resume—know it thoroughly from your education/training through your most recent position.

Review your resume completely and rehearse how you'll describe each role. If you can't recall specific details like study compounds, focus on processes and be honest about what you don't remember.

Below are frequently asked CRA interview questions with sample responses that you can adapt to your personal experience.

THE "TELL ME ABOUT YOURSELF" QUESTION

This open-ended question doesn't provide specific direction, but interviewers typically want to learn about your relevant background for the position. Your response should be a concise overview taking 1-3 minutes.

The best approach is to respond directly and concisely:

Example: "I have more than 5 years experience as a CRA. I graduated from the University of Miami in 2002 with a BS in Biology. While a student, I took courses offered by the Clinical Research department and have stayed current through continuing education. I've worked in Phase I, II, and III trials across cardiovascular, infectious disease, and oncology therapeutic areas. I've conducted numerous pre-study, initiation, routine monitoring, and closeout visits, always following ICH GCP guidelines, adhering to protocols and SOPs, and developing productive relationships with site staff."

After a brief introduction, pause and ask if the interviewer would like you to continue, demonstrating your understanding of conversation dynamics.

WHY DID YOU APPLY FOR THIS POSITION?

This question appears simple but requires careful handling, especially when asked repeatedly by different interviewers. Your enthusiasm must remain consistent throughout.

Research the company thoroughly before interviewing. Visit their website's "About Us" section to understand their mission, values, and strengths. Incorporate this information into your response without being obvious, and practice delivering similar content in varied ways.

Example: "Your company is an industry leader. I'm impressed by your founders' story and persistence. ABC Inc. has a reputation for quality and meeting challenges effectively. I'm seeking challenges within an organization known for collaboration and forward momentum."

"I appreciate your organization's commitment to employee development and internal promotion. This demonstrates a culture where building a long-term career is possible and encouraged."

WHAT ARE YOUR WEAKNESSES?

Avoid the cliché of presenting strengths disguised as weaknesses ("I work too hard"). Instead, present an authentic challenge relevant to the position and explain your solution.

Example: "I previously struggled with organizing project emails, often searching through my inbox inefficiently. I've addressed this by creating project-specific folders where I save all relevant communications. This system saves time and improves my reference efficiency."

"Airport delays used to frustrate me significantly. I've adapted by always traveling with portable work, allowing me to use unexpected downtime productively rather than feeling stalled."

WHAT ARE YOUR SALARY EXPECTATIONS?

Research salary ranges before interviewing using resources like Glassdoor, LinkedIn Salary, and industry reports. Compensation discussions typically occur later in the process, usually with HR after the team decides to hire you.

If asked early in the process, redirect: "What would someone with my background typically earn in this position at your organization?"

If asked later when the interview is progressing well, encourage them to make the first offer: "I'm open to considering your best offer based on the full compensation package."

If they insist on a number, use your research. If the range is $60,000-$70,000, ask for $80,000 and inquire if this aligns with their anticipated range. Avoid providing ranges yourself, as employers typically default to the lower figure.

WHAT AMOUNT OF TIME ARE YOU WILLING TO TRAVEL?

The job posting likely specified expected travel. Unless you have concerns about the stated percentage, confirm your willingness while possibly inquiring about flexibility.

Example: "A 50-70% travel requirement is acceptable. Do you offer flexibility as the relationship develops, allowing for a sustainable balance between travel and home-based work?"

HAVE YOU HAD ANY FORMAL CRA TRAINING?

Organizations want to assess your familiarity with industry practices. While most CROs provide training on their specific processes, candidates with previous training require less onboarding time.

Example: "Yes, I received formal training in my previous two positions. I continue taking continuing education to stay current, particularly on regulatory and GCP guidelines not used daily."

"Yes, I completed an 8-week CRA certification course at Clinical Research Institute. I've continued my education through seminars, webinars, and recently completed NIH's GCP certification program."

WHICH THERAPEUTIC AREAS DO YOU HAVE EXPERIENCE IN?

Align your response with the therapeutic areas mentioned in the job description. If you have relevant experience, discuss it in detail. If your experience is limited, acknowledge this while emphasizing your transferable knowledge.

Example: "I have experience in cardiovascular, infectious disease, and renal therapeutic areas. While my oncology experience focuses primarily on solid tumors, I've studied protocols for hematologic malignancies and believe I can effectively monitor trials in this area based on my foundational knowledge."

DO YOU HAVE ANY QUESTIONS FOR ME?

This classic behavioral question tests your initiative and interest. Never decline to ask questions, even if you've already spoken with multiple interviewers. Prepare thoughtful questions in advance and ask them naturally.

Use this opportunity to highlight your strengths and demonstrate genuine interest in the position.

Example: "Mr. Smith mentioned plans to centralize travel arrangements to allow CRAs to focus on monitoring. What's the timeline for implementing this change?"

"What percentage of time does this position typically involve travel? Will travel be regional, national, or international?"

"How long have you been with Company X, and what attracted you to join the organization?"

"What do you find most rewarding about working at CRO Y?"

GIVE AN EXAMPLE OF AN ISSUE WITH YOUR STUDY TEAM MEMBER AND HOW DID YOU RESOLVE IT?

Interviewers want to understand your conflict resolution approach. Prepare a brief example demonstrating your problem-solving abilities and collaborative mindset.

Example: "After a pre-study visit, I didn't recommend a site due to enrollment concerns. My study team disagreed based on previous positive experiences with the site. I explained that the current study's requirements differed significantly from previous studies, potentially creating enrollment challenges. After thorough discussion, we reached consensus on my assessment."

HOW WOULD YOU RESPOND TO AN AE/SAE?

This question tests your understanding of protocols and guidelines. Adverse events are documented on case report forms and collected during monitoring visits.

Example: "Every clinical trial protocol defines procedures for identifying, documenting, and reporting adverse events. I ensure site personnel receive comprehensive training on these procedures before study initiation."

"Upon learning of an SAE, I immediately verify the site has completed the required SAE form and submitted it within the mandated 24-hour timeframe. I also ensure proper documentation in source records and follow up on any additional information needed."

HOW DO YOU PREPARE SITES FOR DATA SUBMISSION TIMELINES?

Multi-site studies often require synchronized data submission. This question assesses your prioritization skills.

Example: "When managing seven sites on a data submission timeline, I prioritized problematic sites first, resolving data quality issues there before addressing sites with cleaner data. This approach ensured all sites met submission deadlines with high-quality data."

HOW WOULD YOU JUGGLE MULTIPLE PROTOCOLS?

This question evaluates your organizational skills and ability to handle complex workloads.

Example: "I maintain separate digital folders for each protocol with all relevant materials organized within. I create detailed checklists for each monitoring visit and track completion meticulously. This systematic approach ensures nothing important is overlooked despite managing multiple studies."

"I complete monitoring reports promptly, often using travel time productively by writing at airports and during flights. This discipline prevents report backlogs and keeps each protocol's documentation current."

The interview process for CRA positions has evolved to include greater emphasis on technological fluency, remote monitoring capabilities, and risk-based approaches. Being prepared to discuss these aspects of modern clinical research monitoring will further strengthen your candidacy.

CHAPTER 17
GETTING INTO MEDICAL RESIDENCY THROUGH CLINICAL RESEARCH FOR IMGS

f we will be quiet and ready enough, we shall find compensation in every disappointment.

- Henry David Thoreau

Many highly trained professionals migrate to developed nations seeking better opportunities, only to face challenges practicing in their original field. They often work in positions that don't match their training, resulting in diminished job satisfaction, lower compensation, and a loss of valuable talent for society.

However, there is hope—particularly for international medical graduates (IMGs). With the right information, medical professionals can find fulfilling careers that leverage their training and experience while offering six-figure income potential. Clinical research roles, including Clinical Research Associates, Coordinators, and Research Assistants, represent excellent opportunities that typically require only weeks to months of additional training. These programs are fast-paced and comprehensive, with prior medical knowledge significantly easing the transition.

CLINICAL RESEARCH ASSOCIATE (CRA) APPROACH

The CRA or monitor role is particularly well-suited for IMGs. Whether as a career change, an interim position while completing USMLE examinations, or a means to support yourself and your family, working as a CRA offers significant advantages for immigrant physicians.

How to Transition from MD to CRA

Most physicians have encountered clinical research during their medical training or practice. Drug trials are typically organized by therapeutic area, and your experience as a specialist or general practitioner likely provided familiarity with relevant medical domains.

For example, cardiovascular studies might investigate hypertension medications or cholesterol-lowering compounds. Oncology trials might assess tumor responses to new therapies through imaging studies. Your medical background provides valuable context for understanding trial objectives and outcomes.

As outlined in previous chapters, your pathway should include updating your research skills through online programs or certification courses, followed by tailoring your resume to highlight relevant experience.

Avoid using a one-size-fits-all physician resume when applying for clinical research positions. Recruiters lack time to infer transferable skills—you must explicitly demonstrate them. Tailor your resume to each position, highlighting therapeutic areas that align with your clinical experience.

Recruiters look for specific keywords and experiences, so your resume should incorporate terminology from the job posting. Include all research experience, even from medical school, and list all relevant courses and certifications.

Finding a CRA Job

Networking

Networking is crucial for IMGs seeking CRA positions. Many foreign-trained physicians work in clinical research, and CROs value their knowledge, discipline, and understanding of research integrity. Physicians comprehend that even minor protocol deviations can compromise entire studies, similar to how lapses in sterile technique can undermine surgical outcomes.

Referrals

Connect with practicing CRAs to learn about hiring opportunities. Referrals represent one of the most effective pathways into CROs and pharmaceutical companies. A successful CRA can often help secure interviews for qualified candidates they recommend, particularly given the industry's preference for candidates who understand medical concepts and research principles.

Foreign-trained Physician Interview Questions

The interview process for IMGs generally follows the standard format described earlier, including phone and face-to-face interviews. However, you may encounter additional questions related to your physician background:

Why are you transitioning from an MD to CRA?

This question requires careful consideration. Interviewers want to determine if the CRA role represents your career goal or merely a temporary position while pursuing residency. Companies invest resources in training and want assurance of your commitment.

Unless applying for an explicitly temporary position (which most CRA roles are not), emphasize your commitment to clinical research:

Example: "I was actively involved in clinical research in my home country out of genuine interest. Due to monitor shortages, CROs recruited physicians for training programs, which I found engaging. Becoming a CRA in the US allows me to continue contributing to medicine while using my talents in a valuable way."

"After practicing as a physician, I'm drawn to broader opportunities in healthcare. I want to contribute to medical innovation by helping develop new treatments. My medical background ensures I understand trial requirements and can collect accurate, meaningful data."

THE CLINICAL RESEARCH COORDINATOR (CRC) APPROACH

The CRC serves as the operational cornerstone of clinical trials. If leveraging research experience toward residency is your goal, working as a CRC provides valuable patient interaction and physician connections. Some research departments prefer candidates who have passed USMLE exams or achieved ECFMG certification.

CRC positions can be demanding, so investigators generally prefer candidates without competing priorities like board examinations. Tailor your application materials accordingly.

While your hands-on experience will depend on the specific studies and therapeutic areas, the professional network you develop—particularly with the Principal Investigator—provides significant advantages. Although the PI maintains ultimate responsibility for the trial, the CRC drives daily operations and implementation.

If residency is your goal, prioritize research opportunities relevant to your target specialty.

A CRC's responsibilities typically include:

- Ensuring patient safety and welfare throughout the study
- Obtaining proper informed consent from participants
- Organizing and supporting sponsor visits (pre-study, initiation, monitoring, closeout, audits)
- Managing investigational products and supplies
- Completing accurate Case Report Forms (CRFs)
- Resolving data queries within specified timeframes
- Processing and shipping specimens according to protocols and regulations
- Tracking, recording, and reporting Serious Adverse Events (SAEs) to the IRB

RESEARCH ASSISTANT APPROACH

Research Assistant positions may be volunteer or paid roles supporting research studies. You might assist the Principal Investigator or support busy CRCs without a specific job title, taking on tasks as needed—such as preparing forms or collecting vital signs.

This experience provides insights into hospital operations and opportunities to interact with various healthcare professionals. The connections you develop can be invaluable when seeking recommendation letters and referrals for residency applications.

The experience enhances your CV and may satisfy the US hospital experience requirement that some residency programs mandate. Always deliver your best work while remaining alert for opportunities that could strengthen your candidacy.

TIPS FOR LEVERAGING RESEARCH EXPERIENCE FOR RESIDENCY

When completing residency applications and personal statements, highlight your clinical research experience. Emphasize what you've learned and how it has facilitated your integration into the US healthcare system. Demonstrate that you've gained direct experience with patients and physicians, providing an advantage over other international applicants.

Leverage the professional network you've developed through your research experience. These connections can serve as advocates during your residency application process, potentially opening doors to programs and opportunities that might otherwise remain inaccessible.

Clinical research roles offer IMGs valuable pathways to apply their medical knowledge while building credentials and connections that can lead to various career outcomes—whether a permanent position in clinical research or eventual placement in a US medical residency program.

CHAPTER 18
CONCLUSION

A lways bear in mind that your own resolution to succeed is more important than any other.

- Abraham Lincoln

We have come to the conclusion of this book. It is now up to you to take the initiative and claim your CRA position or career. Remember, success is a journey with multiple destinations, separated by time and persistence. If your first attempts don't yield success, learn from each experience and try again.

The clinical research industry continues to evolve rapidly, creating unprecedented opportunities for those willing to prepare and position themselves effectively. As healthcare embraces technological innovation, regulatory complexity, and globalization, the demand for qualified CRAs grows stronger each year.

Several factors make this an especially opportune time to pursue a clinical research career:

1. **Industry growth** - The clinical trials sector continues to expand globally, with increasing numbers of studies across

diverse therapeutic areas.

2. **Remote monitoring options** - The adoption of decentralized trial methodologies has created more flexible work arrangements and expanded geographic opportunities.

3. **Advancing technology** - Electronic data capture systems, risk-based monitoring approaches, and AI-assisted review tools have transformed the monitoring profession.

4. **Regulatory evolution** - Changes in regulatory frameworks have increased the need for knowledgeable professionals who can navigate complex compliance requirements.

5. **Therapeutic specialization** - Expertise in specific medical areas like oncology, rare diseases, or gene therapy can significantly enhance your marketability.

The journey to becoming a successful CRA requires determination, continuous learning, and adaptability. Here are some final recommendations as you move forward:

- **Be patient yet persistent** - Building the necessary experience takes time, but consistent effort yields results.
- **Maintain current knowledge** - Subscribe to industry publications, join professional organizations, and pursue continuing education.
- **Develop your network continuously** - The connections you make today may lead to opportunities tomorrow.
- **Embrace mentorship** - Seek guidance from experienced professionals and, when possible, offer support to others following your path.
- **Document your achievements** - Keep detailed records of your experiences, training, and successes to strengthen future applications.
- **Balance technical and interpersonal skills** - While technical knowledge is essential, your ability to build relationships with site staff often determines your effectiveness.
- **Demonstrate initiative** - In interviews and on the job, show

your willingness to take ownership and solve problems proactively.

Remember that every clinical research professional started some-where, often facing the same "experience paradox" you might be encountering now. With strategic preparation, perseverance, and the practical guidance provided in this book, you can overcome these challenges and build a rewarding career in clinical research monitoring.

Your journey begins with a single step—perhaps reaching out to a potential mentor, applying for that first position, or enrolling in a training program. Whatever your starting point, commit to excellence in everything you do, knowing that each effort brings you closer to your goal of a successful CRA career.

REGULATORY AND GUIDELINES

- FDA Good Clinical Practice Regulations www.fda.gov/regulatory-information/search-fda-guidance-documents/good-clinical-practice
- ICH Guidelines for Good Clinical Practice database.ich.org/sites/default/files/E6_R2_Addendum.pdf
- FDA Form 1572 www.fda.gov/media/71816/download
- The Belmont Report www.hhs.gov/ohrp/regulations-and-policy/belmont-report/index.html
- Declaration of Helsinki www.wma.net/policies-post/wma-declaration-of-helsinki-ethical-principles-for-medical-research-involving-human-subjects/
- EU Clinical Trials Regulation health.ec.europa.eu/medicinal-products/clinical-trials/clinical-trials-regulation-eu-no-5362014_en

PROFESSIONAL ORGANIZATIONS

- Association of Clinical Research Professionals (ACRP) www.acrpnet.org
- Society of Clinical Research Associates (SOCRA) www.socra.org
- Drug Information Association (DIA) www.diaglobal.org
- Clinical Research Society www.clinicalresearchsociety.org
- Clinical Trials Transformation Initiative (CTTI) www.ctti-clinicaltrials.org

TRAINING AND CERTIFICATION

- National Institutes of Health Training Resources www.niaid.nih.gov/research/clinical-research-training-resources
- CITI Program about.citiprogram.org/course/clinical-research-coordinator-crc-basic/

- TransCelerate GCP Training www.transcelerate
biopharmainc.com/initiatives/gcp-training/
- ACRP Certification Programs www.acrpnet.org/
professional-development/certification/
- SOCRA Certification Programs www.socra.org/
certification/

CAREER DEVELOPMENT

- Clinical Research Job Boards www.clinicaljobboard.com
- ACRP Career Center acrp.careerwebsite.com
- LinkedIn Clinical Research Groups www.linkedin.com/
groups/
- Indeed Clinical Research Jobs www.indeed.com/q-Clinical-
Research-jobs.html
- Glassdoor Salary Information www.glassdoor.com/Salaries/
clinical-research-associate-salary-SRCH_KO0,27.htm

INDUSTRY KNOWLEDGE

- CenterWatch - Clinical trials news and information www.
centerwatch.com
- Clinical Leader - Industry trends and best practices www.
clinicalleader.com
- Applied Clinical Trials - Peer-reviewed journal www.
appliedclinicaltrialsonline.com
- Journal of Clinical Research Best Practices
firstclinical.com/journal/
- FDA Bioresearch Monitoring Information www.fda.gov/
science-research/clinical-trials-and-human-subject-
protection/bioresearch-monitoring-information

BOOKS

- "The CRA's Guide to Monitoring Clinical Research" by Karen E. Woodin and John C. Schneider
- "Fundamentals of Clinical Trials" by Lawrence M. Friedman, Curt D. Furberg, David L. DeMets
- "Clinical Trials: Study Design, Endpoints and Biomarkers, Drug Safety, and FDA and ICH Guidelines" by Tom Brody
- "A Guide to Clinical Drug Research" by Adam Cohen and John Posner
- "Principles and Practice of Clinical Research" by John I. Gallin and Frederick P. Ognibene

RESUME AND INTERVIEW RESOURCES

- Action Verbs for Effective Resumes www.bc.edu/content/dam/files/offices/careers/pdf/actionverbsforresumes.pdf
- Interview Preparation Guide for Clinical Research Professionals www.clinicalleader.com/doc/the-clinical-research-job-interview-preparation-guide-0001
- NIH Guide to Resumes & CVs www.training.nih.gov/assets/Writing_CVs_and_Resumes_Handout.pdf
- Mock Interview Practice Platform www.interviewstream.com

TECHNOLOGY AND TOOLS

- Electronic Data Capture Systems Overview www.veeva.com/products/clinical/edc/
- Risk-Based Monitoring Resources www.transcelerate biopharmainc.com/initiatives/risk-based-monitoring/
- Clinical Trial Management Systems Comparison www.capterra.com/clinical-trial-management-software/

ADDITIONAL INFORMATION FOR IMGS

- ECFMG Certification Information www.ecfmg.org/certification/
- Educational Commission for Foreign Medical Graduates www.ecfmg.org
- IMG Resources from the American Medical Association www.ama-assn.org/education/international-medical-education/resources-international-medical-graduates-imgs

ONLINE COMMUNITIES

- Clinical Research Professionals Group on LinkedIn www.linkedin.com/groups/107831/
- r/clinicalresearch on Reddit www.reddit.com/r/clinicalresearch/
- CRA Forums www.craforums.com

ADDITIONAL RESOURCES

GLOSSARY OF COMMON CLINICAL RESEARCH TERMS AND ACRONYMS

AE (Adverse Event): Any untoward medical occurrence in a patient or clinical investigation subject administered a pharmaceutical product, which does not necessarily have a causal relationship with the treatment.

BIMO (Bioresearch Monitoring Program): FDA program that conducts inspections of clinical investigators, sponsors, and IRBs.

CRA (Clinical Research Associate): Professional who monitors clinical trials to ensure compliance with the protocol and regulations.

CRC (Clinical Research Coordinator): Site-based professional who coordinates the daily activities of clinical trials.

CRF/eCRF (Case Report Form/Electronic Case Report Form): Document used to record data from each participating patient in a clinical study.

CRO (Contract Research Organization): Organization contracted by a sponsor to perform one or more research tasks.

CAPA (Corrective and Preventive Action): System for implementing corrective actions and preventive measures in response to identified issues.

DCF (Data Clarification Form): Document used to resolve data discrepancies in clinical trials.

DM (Data Management): Process of collecting, cleaning, and managing subject data in compliance with regulatory standards.

EDC (Electronic Data Capture): Computerized systems designed for the collection of clinical data in electronic format.

GCP (Good Clinical Practice): International ethical and scientific quality standard for designing, conducting, recording, and reporting trials involving human subjects.

ICF (Informed Consent Form): Document that explains the risks and benefits of a clinical trial to potential participants.

ICH (International Council for Harmonisation): Organization that brings together regulatory authorities and pharmaceutical industry to discuss scientific and technical aspects of drug registration.

IND (Investigational New Drug): Application that a drug sponsor must submit to FDA before beginning clinical testing of a new drug in humans.

IP (Investigational Product): A pharmaceutical form of an active ingredient or placebo being tested in a clinical trial.

IRB/IEC (Institutional Review Board/Independent Ethics Committee): Group formally designated to approve, monitor, and review biomedical and behavioral research involving humans.

MedDRA (Medical Dictionary for Regulatory Activities): Standardized medical terminology used for regulatory communication.

PI (Principal Investigator): Person responsible for the conduct of the clinical trial at a trial site.

PV (Pharmacovigilance): Science and activities relating to the detection, assessment, understanding, and prevention of adverse effects or any other drug-related problems.

QA (Quality Assurance): Systematic processes to ensure that a trial is performed and data are generated in compliance with GCP.

QC (Quality Control): Operational techniques and activities undertaken within the quality assurance system to verify that requirements for quality of the trial-related activities have been fulfilled.

RBM (Risk-Based Monitoring): Strategy that focuses monitoring activities on the most critical data elements and processes.

SAE (Serious Adverse Event): Any untoward medical occurrence that results in death, is life-threatening, requires hospitalization, results in disability, or is a congenital anomaly/birth defect.

SDV (Source Data Verification): Comparison of source data with data entered in the CRF/eCRF to ensure accuracy.

SIV (Site Initiation Visit): Meeting to prepare a site to begin enrolling patients in a clinical trial.

SOP (Standard Operating Procedure): Detailed, written instructions to achieve uniformity of the performance of a specific function.

TMF (Trial Master File): Collection of essential documents that allows the conduct of a clinical trial to be evaluated.

UADE (Unanticipated Adverse Device Effect): Any serious adverse effect on health or safety caused by a device that was not identified in the investigational plan.

SAMPLE CRA RESUME TEMPLATE

JANE SMITH, BSN, CRA

123 Research Avenue, Boston, MA 02108 | 555-123-4567 | jane.smith@email.com

PROFESSIONAL SUMMARY

Detail-oriented Clinical Research Associate with 5 years of experience monitoring Phase I-IV clinical trials across multiple therapeutic areas. Strong background in GCP compliance, risk-based monitoring, and site management. Proven track record of building productive relationships with site personnel while ensuring protocol adherence and data integrity.

CERTIFICATIONS

- Certified Clinical Research Associate (CCRA) – ACRP, 2022
- ICH GCP Certification – TransCelerate, 2020 (renewed 2023)
- Human Subject Protection Training – CITI Program, 2023

EDUCATION

Bachelor of Science in Nursing
University of Massachusetts, Boston, MA
Graduated: May 2018

CLINICAL RESEARCH EXPERIENCE

Senior Clinical Research Associate
ABC Clinical Research Organization, Boston, MA
March 2021 – Present

- Monitor 8 active clinical trial sites across 3 Phase III oncology studies
- Conduct pre-study, initiation, interim monitoring, and closeout visits
- Implement risk-based monitoring approaches resulting in 20% reduction in queries
- Train site staff on protocol requirements and GCP guidelines
- Review source documentation to verify data accuracy and protocol compliance
- Identify and address protocol deviations through effective CAPA planning
- Manage investigational product accountability and reconciliation
- Collaborate with multidisciplinary teams to resolve complex site issues

Clinical Research Associate
XYZ Pharmaceuticals, Cambridge, MA
June 2018 – February 2021

- Monitored 5 clinical sites for Phase II cardiovascular studies
- Ensured regulatory compliance and proper documentation maintenance
- Verified informed consent process and subject eligibility

- Tracked and resolved data queries within established timelines
- Reported adverse events according to safety reporting guidelines
- Generated accurate and timely monitoring visit reports

THERAPEUTIC AREAS

Oncology, Cardiovascular, Neurology, Infectious Disease

TECHNICAL SKILLS

- EDC Systems: Medidata Rave, Oracle Clinical, Veeva Vault EDC
- CTMS: Medidata CTMS, Oracle Siebel CTMS
- Microsoft Office Suite (Excel, Word, PowerPoint, Outlook)
- Remote Monitoring Platforms: Veeva SiteVault, Florence eBinders

PROFESSIONAL AFFILIATIONS

- Association of Clinical Research Professionals (ACRP)
- Drug Information Association (DIA)

LANGUAGES

- English (Native)
- Spanish (Professional Proficiency)

EMERGING TRENDS IN CLINICAL RESEARCH

Decentralized Clinical Trials (DCTs)

The COVID-19 pandemic accelerated the adoption of decentralized approaches to clinical trials, fundamentally changing how studies are conducted. DCTs move activities traditionally performed at research sites to patients' homes or local healthcare facilities through technologies like telemedicine, mobile health applications, wearable devices, and direct-to-patient shipment of investigational products.

For CRAs, this evolution demands new competencies:

- Remote monitoring skills
- Proficiency with virtual oversight platforms
- Understanding of digital data streams
- Ability to verify protocol compliance in virtual environments
- Knowledge of regulations specific to decentralized approaches

The hybrid model—combining elements of traditional site-based and decentralized approaches—has emerged as the predominant paradigm. This approach allows protocols to be customized based on therapeutic area, patient population, and regulatory environment.

Artificial Intelligence and Machine Learning

AI and ML are transforming clinical research across multiple dimensions:

1. **Monitoring and Quality Management**:
   - Automated data review to identify anomalies and potential fraud
   - Predictive analytics to focus monitoring efforts on high-risk sites
   - Pattern recognition to detect safety signals earlier
2. **Protocol Development**:
   - Optimization of inclusion/exclusion criteria
   - Identification of potential recruitment challenges
   - Simulation of trial outcomes based on design parameters
3. **Patient Recruitment and Retention**:
   - Matching algorithms to identify eligible patients from electronic health records
   - Predictive models for dropout risk

- Personalized engagement strategies based on behavioral
  data

While these technologies enhance efficiency, they require CRAs to develop new analytical skills and understand how to interpret AI-generated insights alongside traditional monitoring approaches.

Risk-Based Quality Management (RBQM)

The evolution from traditional 100% source data verification to risk-based approaches represents a fundamental shift in monitoring strategy. RBQM focuses resources on areas of highest risk to patient safety and data integrity through:

1. **Risk Assessment**: Systematic evaluation of protocol-specific risks
2. **Risk Control**: Implementation of targeted mitigation strategies
3. **Risk Review**: Ongoing evaluation of risk indicators and effectiveness of controls
4. **Risk Communication**: Transparent documentation and reporting of risk management activities

For CRAs, RBQM requires deeper analytical thinking, greater focus on centralized data review, and the ability to adapt monitoring plans based on emerging risk patterns.

Patient-Centricity and Diversity

Recognition of the importance of diverse trial populations has led to significant changes in trial design and execution:

1. **Protocol Development**: Designing studies with reduced participant burden
2. **Site Selection**: Expanding beyond traditional academic centers to community settings
3. **Eligibility Criteria**: Removing unnecessary restrictions that limit diversity
4. **Patient Engagement**: Including patient input throughout the research process

CRAs play a critical role in implementing these approaches through site training, community engagement, and ensuring inclusive recruitment strategies.

Regulatory Evolution

Regulatory frameworks continue to evolve in response to technological and methodological innovations:

1. **FDA's Digital Health Technologies Guidance**
2. **EMA's Qualification of Novel Methodologies**
3. **ICH E6(R3) Development**: Focusing on quality-by-design principles
4. **Real-World Evidence Acceptance**: Increasing use of observational data to support regulatory decisions

Successful CRAs must stay current with these regulatory developments while maintaining core competencies in GCP and human subject protection.

CASE STUDIES: SUCCESSFUL CAREER TRANSITIONS INTO CLINICAL RESEARCH

From Nursing to Senior CRA: Sarah's Journey

Background: Sarah worked as an ICU nurse for eight years before becoming interested in clinical research after her hospital participated in a COVID-19 treatment trial.

Challenge: While Sarah had strong clinical knowledge, she lacked formal research experience and struggled to make her nursing experience relevant to CRA positions.

Strategy:

1. She completed an online Clinical Research Certificate program while continuing to work
2. Volunteered to assist her hospital's research department on weekends
3. Joined ACRP and attended networking events

4. Created a resume highlighting transferable skills: attention to detail, protocol adherence, patient assessment, and documentation

First Position: Sarah secured a role as a Clinical Research Coordinator at her hospital's research department, managing oncology trials.

Progression: After 18 months as a CRC, she applied for an in-house CRA position at a mid-sized CRO, highlighting her direct trial experience.

Current Status: Three years later, Sarah is now a Senior CRA specializing in oncology trials, earning 40% more than her previous nursing position with better work-life balance.

Key Insight: "My nursing background gives me an advantage in understanding the clinical implications of protocol requirements. When I discuss adverse event reporting with site staff, I can relate to their challenges while still ensuring compliance."

From Academic Researcher to CRA: Michael's Transition

Background: Michael completed a PhD in molecular biology and worked as a postdoctoral researcher for three years before realizing academic career prospects were limited.

Challenge: While knowledgeable about scientific principles, Michael lacked understanding of regulatory requirements and clinical operations.

Strategy:

1. Took GCP training and earned SOCRA certification
2. Leveraged university connections to shadow an experienced CRA
3. Highlighted transferable skills: protocol development, data analysis, and attention to detail
4. Accepted a lower starting salary to break into the field

First Position: Entry-level CRA at a large CRO focusing on Phase I studies, where his scientific background was particularly valuable.

Progression: Quickly advanced to CRA II within 18 months based on performance and therapeutic expertise.

Current Status: Now a Lead CRA managing a team of junior monitors for complex gene therapy trials.

Key Insight: "My scientific background helps me understand complex mechanisms of action and anticipate potential safety concerns. When sponsors explain their products, I can engage at a deeper level and translate that understanding into effective monitoring."

From International Medical Graduate to Clinical Research Leader: Dr. Patel's Story

Background: Dr. Patel was a practicing physician in India before immigrating to the United States. Despite extensive clinical experience, residency positions were extremely competitive.

Challenge: Needed to find a healthcare role that valued his medical knowledge while building U.S. experience.

Strategy:

1. Volunteered at an academic medical center's research department
2. Completed ECFMG certification while gaining research experience
3. Networked with other IMGs who had successfully transitioned to research
4. Tailored his resume to emphasize therapeutic expertise rather than clinical practice

First Position: Clinical Research Coordinator at a university hospital managing diabetes studies.

Progression: Moved to a CRA position at a pharmaceutical company within two years, then to Senior CRA.

Current Status: Now serves as a Clinical Sciences Director overseeing multiple studies and providing medical input on protocol development.

Key Insight: "My medical training allows me to spot potential safety issues that might be missed by others. When reviewing adverse events, I can quickly assess causality and importance, which sponsors particularly value."

INTERVIEW PREPARATION CHECKLIST

Two Weeks Before

- Research the company (history, pipeline, therapeutic focus)
- Study the job description and identify key requirements
- Update your resume to align with specific position requirements
- Prepare a list of your monitoring experience by therapeutic area
- Review GCP guidelines and relevant regulations
- Research typical salary ranges for the position
- Gather information about the company culture (Glassdoor, LinkedIn)
- Prepare questions to ask the interviewer

One Week Before

- Conduct mock interviews with a friend or mentor
- Review common interview questions and prepare responses
- Practice explaining gaps in employment or career transitions
- Create a tracking document for consistent responses across multiple interviews
- Prepare examples of how you've handled challenging situations
- Review your monitoring experience metrics (# of sites, studies, etc.)
- Verify all certification dates and training details
- Select appropriate professional attire for in-person interviews

Day Before

- Confirm interview time and format (phone, video, in-person)

- For video interviews: Test your equipment and internet connection
- For in-person: Confirm location and estimated travel time
- Review your notes on the company and position
- Print copies of your resume and reference list
- Prepare a professional notebook and pen for notes
- Review your prepared questions for the interviewer
- Get adequate rest and prepare mentally

Interview Day

- Arrive early (15-20 minutes) for in-person interviews
- Log in 5-10 minutes early for virtual interviews
- Bring copies of your resume, certifications, and references
- Have your tracking document nearby for phone interviews
- Turn phone to silent mode
- Take brief notes during the interview
- Collect business cards or contact information
- Ask about next steps in the hiring process

Post-Interview

- Send a thank-you email within 24 hours
- Document the questions asked for future reference
- Follow up after the timeframe mentioned for next steps
- Update your tracking document with responses given
- Reflect on areas for improvement in future interviews

SAMPLE ANSWERS TO ADDITIONAL INTERVIEW QUESTIONS

"How do you handle protocol deviations at a site?"

Strong Answer: "When I identify a protocol deviation, my first step is to thoroughly document the issue and assess its potential impact on patient safety and data integrity. I then discuss it with the site staff to understand the root cause and ensure they recognize why it's a deviation.

For minor deviations, I work with the site to implement corrective actions immediately and develop preventive measures to avoid recurrence. This might include additional training or process improvements.

For significant deviations, I promptly notify the project manager and sponsor according to escalation procedures. I ensure the site completes any required reporting to the IRB and help them develop a comprehensive CAPA plan.

In a recent cardiovascular study, I identified inconsistent ECG timing at one site. Rather than simply noting the deviation, I worked with the coordinator to develop a timing checklist that was incorporated into their source documents. This simple tool eliminated further deviations and was eventually adopted across all sites in the study."

"How do you prioritize when monitoring multiple studies simultaneously?"

Strong Answer: "I prioritize my monitoring activities using a risk-based approach. First, I assess each site based on factors like enrollment rate, previous issues, protocol complexity, and upcoming milestones.

I maintain a comprehensive tracking system that flags time-sensitive activities like safety reporting deadlines, upcoming database locks, and required follow-up on previous findings. This allows me to allocate my time effectively across all studies.

When managing competing priorities, I communicate proactively with project managers to ensure alignment on expectations. I'm transparent about potential resource constraints and suggest solutions rather than simply highlighting problems.

For instance, when simultaneously managing an oncology study approaching database lock and a new site initiation in another study, I negotiated a slight adjustment to the initiation timeline to ensure quality wouldn't be compromised in either activity. This transparent approach has helped me successfully manage up to four complex studies simultaneously."

"How do you establish rapport with site staff while maintaining your oversight role?"

Strong Answer: "Building productive relationships with site staff requires balancing partnership with oversight responsibilities. I approach each site with respect for their expertise while clearly communicating expectations.

During initial visits, I focus on understanding their processes and challenges rather than immediately highlighting issues. This demonstrates that I value their perspective and am there to support their success, not just point out problems.

I establish myself as a resource by responding promptly to questions and proactively sharing information that helps them perform better. When issues arise, I frame feedback constructively, focusing on solutions rather than blame.

In one challenging situation, I inherited a site with historically poor relationships with previous CRAs. Rather than continuing the adversarial dynamic, I scheduled extra time during my first visit to understand their frustrations. By acknowledging legitimate challenges and collaboratively developing solutions, I transformed the relationship while still ensuring compliance improved significantly."

"How do you adapt your monitoring approach to different therapeutic areas?"

Strong Answer: "Each therapeutic area presents unique monitoring considerations that require adaptable approaches. In oncology trials, I pay particular attention to SAE reporting and proper assessment of tumor response criteria, which often involve complex imaging requirements.

For CNS studies, I focus on ensuring consistent administration of subjective assessments and verifying rater qualifications. With cardiovascular trials, I emphasize proper handling of ECGs, vital signs timing, and concomitant medication documentation.

Beyond disease-specific considerations, I adapt to the patient population characteristics. Pediatric studies require careful verification of age-appropriate consent/assent, while geriatric studies often involve monitoring for polypharmacy issues.

My approach is to deeply understand the protocol's scientific objectives and potential risks to both patients and data integrity. This understanding informs where I focus my monitoring efforts while maintaining comprehensive oversight of regulatory compliance and patient safety across all therapeutic areas."

"How do you stay current with evolving regulations and industry practices?"

Strong Answer: "Staying current with regulations and industry best practices is essential in our rapidly evolving field. I maintain memberships in ACRP and DIA, which provide regular updates through publications and webinars.

I've established a weekly routine of reviewing key regulatory websites, including FDA and EMA guidance updates. I subscribe to several industry newsletters that summarize regulatory changes and emerging trends.

Beyond passive consumption, I participate in professional forums and discussion groups where practical implications of new guidelines are debated. This helps me understand not just what is changing, but how those changes should be implemented.

I also leverage internal resources, participating in company training programs and contributing to our organization's working groups on topics like risk-based monitoring implementation. This collaborative approach ensures I'm not just aware of changes but can effectively apply them in my monitoring activities.

For example, when ICH GCP E6(R2) was implemented, I didn't just complete required training—I volunteered to help develop our company's updated monitoring procedures, which deepened my understanding of the practical applications of the revised guidelines."

MAINTAINING WORK-LIFE BALANCE IN A TRAVEL-HEAVY ROLE

Strategic Planning for Sustainable Travel

Optimize Territory Management

- Request geographically clustered sites when possible
- Schedule consecutive site visits in the same region to minimize travel days

- Identify hub airports with multiple direct connections to reduce transit time

Establish Travel Boundaries

- Define your non-negotiable personal time requirements
- Communicate availability constraints respectfully but clearly
- Consider limiting overnight travel to 2-3 nights per week when possible

Leverage Remote Monitoring Options

- Advocate for hybrid monitoring approaches when appropriate
- Propose alternating on-site and remote visits for stable sites
- Use central monitoring findings to focus on-site time on critical areas

Self-Care During Travel
Maintain Physical Well-being

- Pack exercise clothes and use hotel fitness facilities
- Research healthy meal options near your hotel in advance
- Establish a consistent sleep routine despite changing time zones
- Stay hydrated, especially during flights

Manage Mental Health

- Schedule regular check-ins with family and friends
- Develop decompression rituals for hotel evenings
- Consider mindfulness or meditation practices for travel days
- Set boundaries on work hours while traveling

Create Portable Comforts

- Develop a travel kit with familiar items from home
- Establish consistent routines regardless of location
- Consider noise-canceling headphones for flights and hotel work

Home Life Integration
Quality vs. Quantity Time

- Plan meaningful activities during home periods
- Be fully present during non-work time (limit email checking)
- Create special traditions for return days

Leverage Technology

- Use video calls for meaningful connections with family
- Participate in important events remotely when necessary
- Share your travel schedule with family to manage expectations

Home Base Efficiency

- Develop systems for quick unpacking/repacking
- Consider meal preparation services to reduce domestic burdens
- Establish low-maintenance household arrangements

Career Sustainability Strategies
Negotiate Effectively

- Discuss travel expectations clearly during hiring process
- Revisit travel requirements during performance reviews
- Propose innovative solutions that benefit both you and the company

Career Progression Planning

- Investigate less travel-intensive roles as career advancement options
- Develop skills for in-house positions requiring field experience
- Consider specialization in therapeutic areas with sites in your region

Preventing Burnout

- Recognize early warning signs of travel fatigue
- Use vacation time strategically for true disconnection
- Consider sabbaticals or reduced schedules during intensive life periods

Success Story: Elena's Balanced Approach After experiencing burnout from 80% travel as a CRA, Elena implemented several changes:

1. Negotiated a territory limited to a 300-mile radius of her home
2. Developed expertise in remote monitoring technologies
3. Proposed and implemented a 3-weeks-on, 1-week-off travel schedule
4. Created a home office optimized for productive remote work days

These changes allowed her to continue advancing in her career while reducing overnight travel to approximately 40%, demonstrating that with strategic planning and clear communication, sustainable work-life balance is achievable even in travel-intensive CRA roles.

ABOUT THE AUTHOR

J.P. Holdasham has guided countless professionals into successful clinical research careers since publishing the first edition of this guide in 2012. Combining industry knowledge with a straightforward approach to career development, J.P. has helped readers overcome the "experience paradox" that challenges many aspiring CRAs. Through practical, results-focused strategies, J.P. continues to support life science graduates, nurses, and international medical graduates in launching rewarding careers in clinical research monitoring.

www.ingramcontent.com/pod-product-compliance
Lightning Source LLC
Chambersburg PA
CBHW030531210326
41597CB00014B/1104